General Editor's Preface

Contrasts in History is designed for use by students preparing for G.C.E. O Level and S.C.E. O Grade examinations. The volumes in the series could also be used for work of a more advanced nature.

Although the need to provide a narrative framework is not overlooked, the real intention is that each volume, by identifying and analysing problems, should introduce readers to the complexities of historical personalities and situations.

It is hoped that a series which illustrates the many-sided nature of events and periods, examines contrasts within and between societies, demonstrates the interplay of change and continuity, and seeks to create an awareness of differing interpretations, will help to build up a sense of the past and encourage the development of thinking skills.

DUNCAN MACINTYRE

Acknowledgments

The author and publisher wish to thank the following for permission to reproduce the photographs listed below.

The Illustrated London News: *pages (vi), 41, 60 (foot)*
Harrogate Art Gallery: *page 11*
City of Manchester Art Galleries: *page 17*
The Mansell Collection: *page 19*
Punch: *pages 23, 49, 60 (top)*
The Glasgow Collection: *page 47*
The Annan Collection: *page 63*

Contents

First, Second and Third Class passengers on their way to the Epsom Races, 1847.

Part One
The Two Nations

1. Upper and Middle Classes

From the beginnings of history there have been rich and poor. The Roman patrician lived very differently from his slave, the lord of the manor from his serf, king from commoner. But it was in the nineteenth century that class consciousness first became a powerful force, classes of society became defined and the position of people within society recognizable. The changes brought about by the Industrial Revolution were largely responsible for this.

Classes did not, however, emerge *clearly* defined in the early nineteenth century—it took time and experience for their identities to evolve. We eventually find three groups emerging, not two, each so diverse that we refer to them all in the plural—upper classes, middle classes, lower classes. We shall see how wide each class was, what a variety of situations and circumstances was included in each, making it impossible to generalize, leaving us only to draw tentative conclusions from available evidence.

In the early nineteenth century a man's position in society could be determined by a number of things, including income, family and occupation. For membership of the upper classes, however, the ownership of land was essential. Two groups (within which there was a wide range of incomes) met this requirement: the landed aristocracy and the landed gentry.

Although there were exceptions to the general rule, the gentry could be said to number about 3,000, having an annual income of between £1,000 and £10,000, with perhaps 1,000 to 10,000 acres. The landed aristocracy on the other hand, some 300 or so, enjoyed incomes exceeding £10,000 per annum, with the Dukes of Northumberland at the top of the scale able to reckon on about £130,000, and the Dukes of Portland about £100,000. The distribution of titles throughout this group varied, but most of them would have a house and estate in the country and own or hire a house in London for the Season.

During the nineteenth century many landowners added vast sums to their income by exploiting mineral resources and raising rents from urban property. Most were also affected by railway development— with some investing in railway building, some being paid for permitting the line to cross their land, and others being compensated handsomely for withdrawing their objections to the railway's proximity to their homes. Although some incurred local resentment by refusing to bring in the line, and therefore losing the resulting benefits, outright opposition was rare, largely because the value of farm land was increased by access to a railway:

> . . . about 7% [on the rent] would be a moderate estimate of the benefit that all the land within five miles of a railway station . . . would receive.[1]

The size and splendour of an upper-class establishment depended on the income of the owner, and of course the life style was based on the work of servants. A large household might employ forty or fifty indoor servants, while a smaller house with say seven bedrooms could be run by a staff of six.

Although one observer could argue that

> . . . the liberty which endears factory life to both lads and lasses is in strong contrast with the restraints of domestic service,[2]

servants did have certain advantages which compensated for their long hours of work and relatively low wages. They had, for example, a degree of security, unless they were dismissed "without a character". The quality of food and lodging could vary but it was often very good in an upper-class house; in addition, girls were given the chance of a good domestic training which improved their marriage prospects.

> In nothing was the contrast between wealth and poverty more obvious than in food. House, dress or manners might still be a misleading test of income in 1850, but a man's dinner-table instantly announced his standard of living to the world at large.[3]

French cookery and service were the fashion by the 1840s. Banquets were magnificent affairs, the food being reported in more detail by the press than the speeches! At a banquet in Liverpool in 1855, Nathaniel Hawthorne ate "turtle soup, salmon, woodcock, oyster patties . . ." but also found

> the exchange pavement densely thronged with people of all ages and all manner of dirt and rags. They were waiting for soup tickets and waiting very patiently, too—only patience and meekness in their faces.

He added that this seemed to indicate

> an insolence of riches and prosperity which will, one day or another, have a downfall.[4]

Victorian appetites must have been bigger than ours! In 1853 Hawthorne gave an opinion on Englishwomen:

As a general rule, they are not very desirable in their youth and, in many instances, become perfectly grotesque after middle age; so massive and not seemingly with pure fat, but with solid beef. You think of them as composed of sirloins and with broad and thick steaks on their immense rears.[4]

Photographs of the period show he was not mistaken in his view!

In matters of dress, only the upper class could afford to be leaders of fashion. In 1834

the diameter of the fashionable ladies at the moment is about three yards,[5a]

while in 1842, according to the diary of Caroline Clive,

Lady Aylesbury wears forty-eight yards of material in each of her gowns.[5b]

By 1860 a dress over a crinoline was reported to be ten yards round the hem. (A crinoline, incidentally, was among the lost property at the Great Exhibition!)

Appropriate jewellery and accessories were, of course, worn. *The Family Friend* in September 1858 analysed the cost of a young lady's ensemble under the heading "The Cost of a Modern Belle". Items may be abstracted as follows:

Diamond head-dress	£500— 0—0
Brooch—gold and enamel	30—10—0
Lilac satin slip	10—10—0
2 skirts of white lace	31—10—0
6 bows of purple ribbon	15—0
8 yards silver fringe (9″ deep)	11—11—0
Belt and clasp	30— 0—0
Kid gloves and bracelet	22— 5—6
Slippers of silk and satin	14—6
	£637—16—0 [6]

Men's clothes, by mid-century, were generally sober in colour and in style and changed little over the next fifty years. It was argued that

a gentleman of the present nineteenth century, attired for the gayest evening party, would, apart from his jewellery, be equally presentable at the most sorrowful funeral.[7]

The upper classes were obviously those with most time to spare for leisure activities. Some men were devoted to sport, some to politics. Unless politics or business demanded constant presence in

London—and railways made travel easy—much time would be spent in the country, where guests often joined the family. Shooting in August, hunting in the winter, the Season in London, summer holidays by the sea or abroad—this constituted a typical year.

During the Season, there were balls, theatres, dinner parties, riding and driving in Hyde Park, exhibitions, picnics—lavish entertainments of all sorts. It was also the time for playing the marriage market. Parents, after all, had daughters whom they wished to marry off. Lord Verulam wrote in his diary:

> *I suppose the dash will be continued until the three young ladies are married, after which the necessity for entertaining will not be so great.*[8a]

As for the sons, they sought wealthy wives. An aunt recorded that she would like to see her nephew

> *married to a nice girl with a good fortune. . . . I should be very sorry for you to marry for money, but a nice wife with it would not be bad.*[8b]

This aunt thoughtfully recommended a young lady with £15,000 a year!

The nobility was not averse to marrying its sons to girls with fortunes originally made in banking or even trade. This trend continued in the late nineteenth century when they cast their eyes across the Atlantic. American heiresses (Winston Churchill's mother was one) were much sought after because they brought new blood and U.S. dollars into the British aristocracy.

Children of the Victorian upper classes generally wore clothes which were copies, in miniature, of adult styles. They spent their time in the nursery, in the care of nursemaids and nannies, and later in the school-room, ruled, if she had the personality to do it, by a governess. Boys might have a tutor, often a clergyman. The happiness of the children depended largely upon the servants appointed to care for them, and they could vary much in character and ability.

> *Is it not monstrous,* remarked an observer, *that while a lady will not give her dress to be made to anyone but a first-class dressmaker, she will give her children to be educated by a second- or third-rate governess?*[9]

A governess usually earned about £30 a year. Charlotte Bronte, in her last post, was paid £20 a year, less £4 for washing. She wrote:

> *I used to think I should like to be in the stir of grand folks' society but I have had enough of it—it is dreary work to look on and listen.*[10]

Children could plague those in charge of them. Governesses often received no backing from parents in their efforts to discipline their pupils. Charlotte wrote to her sister Emily in June 1839:

In the Bosom of his Family.

The Children are constantly with me. As for correcting them, I quickly found that was out of the question; they are to do as they like. A complaint to the mother only brings black looks on myself and unjust partial excuses to screen the children. . . .[10]

Governesses lived in constant fear of dismissal and of old age.

On the whole, the Victorians displayed little sentimentality towards children, who were often housed in unheated rooms and fed on "wholesome" and unappetising food. Religion, however, was one aspect of education which received heavy emphasis. In 1844, Queen Victoria wrote a memorandum on the religious training of her eldest child, the Princess Royal:

I am quite clear that she should be taught to have a great reverence for God and for religion but that she should have the feeling of devotion and love which our Heavenly Father encourages His Earthly children to have for Him, and not one of fear and trembling; and that thoughts of death and an after-life should not be represented in an alarming and forbidding view. . . .[11]

In contrast, many children were brought up on

Divine and Moral Songs for Children,

of which the following is an example:

Have you not heard, what dreadful plagues,   *What heavy guilt upon him lies!*
Are threatened by the Lord,   *How cursed is his name!*
To him who breaks his father's laws,   *The ravens shall pick out his eyes*
Or mocks his mother's word?   *And eagles eat the same.*[12]

As a result, a sensitive child could reflect:

Now and then, believing, in obedience to my mother's assurances and the solemn prayers of the ministers about me, that I was a child of Hell, and a lost and miserable sinner, I used to have accesses of terror, and fancy that I should surely wake next morning in everlasting flames.[13]

Men in a wide variety of occupations called themselves "middle-class", and often rich merchants and industrialists lived in grander style than many an impoverished peer. From the richer clergy and London doctors, successful writers and artists, university professors and public school headmasters, down through yeoman farmers, prosperous tradesmen, attorneys, mill-managers, to teachers and clerks —all those and many others claimed a place in the ranks of the middle classes, becoming more self-assertive from the 1820s on. Lord Brougham could call them in 1831

the wealth and intelligence of the country and the glory of the British name.

For inclusion in the ranks of the middle classes, a steady and, if possible, increasing income, derived from non-manual labour in business or a profession, was necessary, with a possible minimum of £100 a year. The nature of the official records makes it impossible to determine accurately the details of mid-nineteenth-century middle-class incomes. Nevertheless, it seems definite that the numbers of the middle class increased vastly in comparison with the increase in population, and that the size of middle-class incomes increased, on the whole, well beyond the increase in prices of the period. Thus REAL incomes rose between 1851 and 1871, and the buying power of the middle classes increased. Many of them became accustomed to a higher standard of living. It is arguable that, in order to maintain this higher standard of living, the middle and upper classes decided to limit the size of their families.

	1851	1871	% increase
Total number of incomes over £200 taxed under Schedule E*	19,044	37,192	95.3
Males in employment (aged 20 and over)	4,423,000	6,676,700	24.6
Total population	20,879,000	26,158,000	25.2

*Income from any public office or employment[6]

6

In most British cities the prosperous middle class moved westward or south, to avoid the smoke and grime of industrial districts carried by the prevailing winds. In the centre of towns there was an *absence of the higher classes, who, like the aristocracy, do not live in the town. The district in which a large proportion of the wealth of the town is created and where the hands which created it live is one where none of the employers, the more educated and refined reside, who can avoid it.*
This, of course, led to
the wider separation of classes in great towns—a separation produced by the increase of commercial wealth.

Since only the upper middle class were "carriage folk", most people travelled to work by public transport, and items such as railway season tickets began to appear in household budgets. From this time dates the growth of suburbia, often governed by the proximity of a railway line.

Income dictated the size of house. In order of desirability and cost came (1) a villa in its own grounds; (2) a semi-detached villa; (3) a terraced house. Flats were not fashionable until the 1870s, except in Scotland where all classes were accustomed to flat-dwelling and the style of tenement building indicated class distinction.

The particular house, in turn, required a specific number of servants—for the owners' comfort and to demonstrate their status. Seebohm Rowntree believed that the keeping of servants marked the middle class off from the working class.

At the lowest level, daily help only was occasionally employed. Then a maid-of-all-work/general servant, with a girl to help on occasions, would cost £9–£14 a year. At an income of £300 per annum, a second servant was possible—a nurserymaid or housemaid at £8–£12. Next came a cook, at £14–£30, and all ranges of household work were covered. To be complete, a household was taken to require three female servants—thus an income of at least £400 per annum was to be aimed at. Only at the level of £600–£700 was it considered possible to afford a carriage. Servants' wages varied according to age, experience and duties.

The average age at marriage of "gentlemen" between 1840 and 1870 was 29. Much was made of "keeping up appearances". *How to Woo, When, And To Whom* (1855) declared that worldly circumstances *at the time of marriage . . . should present a reasonable probability of increase, or at the least, of a firm certainty;*[6]
and according to the *Guardian*, in an article of 27 January 1858 entitled "Morals and Manners":

People in these days have an acute sense of the duty of not marrying . . .
without a competent support. . . .[6]

A lively correspondence flourished in *The Times* in 1858 on whether or not a man could marry on £300 a year. Obviously, much depended upon individuals' ideas of necessities and luxuries. *The Times* of 2 July 1861 maintained that

newly-married couples expect to begin where their fathers and mothers ended.[6]

To do that, they had to postpone marriage.

But some men did not marry at all. In 1851 there were 100 men to 96 women but of every 100 men, 26 were unmarried at age 30, 18 unmarried at age 35 and 11 at 50. Almost 40% of all women in England and Wales between 20 and 44 were unmarried. This figure may include the working-class women who were married in all but name but could not afford the licence fee. In the 1880s, a new rector in a country parish, scandalized by the numbers "living in sin", persuaded a local benefactress to pay the fees so that many old couples, nearing the stage of a golden wedding, could at long last become respectably married.

While no blame attached to single men, the position of a spinster without money of her own was unenviable. Jane Austen's Emma said:

A single woman of good fortune is always respectable[14]

but Jane herself remarked:

Single women have a dreadful propensity for being poor[15]

and career prospects for women only began in the 1870s.

From the 1820s on, there was an increasing output of books, pamphlets and magazine articles on domestic matters, directed mainly at the middle classes, because many wives, totally submissive to their parents before marriage, had no idea of the value of money—David Copperfield's Dora was Dickens' comment on this. All the books dealt with budgeting, some with cookery. The most famous and comprehensive of all was *The Book of Household Management* which first appeared in 1861, written by Mrs Isabella Beeton, who died in childbed in 1865, aged 28. In 1845, however, appeared Eliza Acton's *Modern Cookery for Private Families*, dedicated to "the young Housekeepers of England". Miss Acton made some astute pronouncements in her Preface:

It cannot be denied that an improved system of practical domestic cookery, and a better knowledge of its first principles, are still much needed in this country; where, from ignorance or from mismanagement in their preparation, the daily waste of excellent provisions almost exceeds belief.

8

It is not so much cookery books which we need half so much as cooks really trained to a knowledge of their duties and suited ... to families of different grades.

It is a popular error to imagine that what is called good cookery is adapted only to the establishments of the wealthy, and that it is beyond the reach of those that are not affluent ... it is of the utmost consequence that the food which is served at the more simply supplied tables of the middle classes should be well and skilfully prepared, particularly as it is from these classes that the men principally come to whose indefatigable industry, high intelligence and active genius, we are mainly indebted for our advancement in science, in art, in literature and in general civilization.[16]

It is interesting to note how many commodities, which previously would have had to be made at home, appeared to be available in the shops—preserves, sauces, even bread. A variety of fruits was obviously being imported by mid-century.

All Miss Acton's "receipts" (recipes) are clearly and simply explained, with the list of ingredients and cooking time at the end. She does not give cost, unlike Mrs Beeton who tells us, for instance, that, at 1s. (5p) a pint, the cream for a trifle, with sugar, lemon, white of egg and a glass of sherry added, will cost 1s. 9d. (9p)! It will also take *one hour* to whip!

No set percentage of income spent on food can be quoted. It varied in different ranks of the middle classes and according to price fluctuation.

A HOUSEKEEPING ACCOUNT BOOK should invariably be kept, and kept punctually and precisely,[17]
advised Mrs Beeton and many housewives did keep careful budgets, aided by the *Domestic Account Book* and other similar publications, ruled off and printed with headings like "Bread", "Flour", "Meat", "Fish", "Servants' Wages", "Wearing Apparel". Such account books, kept by the wife and submitted for her husband's inspection, would show how every penny had been expended.

It seemed that the lower income groups spent proportionately more on certain items and thus had to cut back on others. Certainly, as a family prospered, their meals became larger, more varied and more ambitious. Alexis Soyer, the progressive chef at the Reform Club, who installed a gas cooker there and later organized soup kitchens during the Irish famine and reformed the arrangements for feeding the troops in the Crimea, traces in his book *The Modern Housewife* the rising standards of a Mrs B. of St John's Wood, from her husband's early days as a small shopkeeper when she served Sunday's Roast Beef as Hash on Monday to the days of his prosperity when

our bill of fare consists of something like the following. One Soup or Fish, generally alternate—One Remove, either Joint or Poultry—One Entrée— Two Vegetables—Pudding or Tart—A little Dessert.[18]

An elegant dinner party once a month gave the middle-class hostess the chance to emulate, to the best of her ability, the life of the upper classes.

In dress, middle-class women strove to copy the fashions worn by their superiors, though often in less expensive materials and harsher colours. After the invention in 1856 of aniline dyes, some harsh, crude colours were produced which were softened by gaslight but later found to be too garish by the stronger electric lighting. Two shades were called "magenta" and "solferino" after the bloody battles in 1859 in Italy.

French fashion magazines had existed for some time but in the 1850s half a dozen new publications appeared, including *The English-woman's Domestic Magazine* and *The Ladies' Treasury*. In 1850, *World of Fashion*, a monthly magazine costing 1s., began to issue free dress patterns. Dresses could also be bought partly made up, so that dressmakers could complete them quickly after one fitting. Probably ready-made dresses were available from the 1840s, though not in popular use for long after that. The opening of the department stores, from the late 1850s on, made shopping much easier.

In bringing up their children, mid-Victorian parents were not bound by any compulsion to have them educated. Thus the education of middle-class children depended upon various factors—where they lived, what their parents could afford and their regard for learning. The well-off followed the upper-class pattern of teaching at home. Others made use of private schools or the local grammar school, if such existed, for their sons—schooling for girls was not considered important. The quality of all types of schools varied very much. Anybody could put a sign up and start a school—there was no inspection and no set qualifications for staff. By mid-century, however, an increasing demand arose for something better and the public school movement gathered momentum.

Children were certainly not spoiled in the nineteenth century. Usually, they rose in an unheated nursery and washed in cold water. Breakfasts of bread and milk, dinners of boiled mutton and milk pudding were the rule, while jam or cake for tea was a special treat. Children's books showed what high standards of behaviour were

Many Happy Returns by W. P. Frith shows a typically large, well-to-do family in their comfortable dining-room. Notice there are three generations present —and how many children?

expected—complete obedience and utter truthfulness amongst other virtues. Too much play would encourage idleness, which was a sin. Punishments were often cruel. Physically, a child might be beaten or deprived of food. Perhaps more damaging were the psychological effects of solitary confinement, of being sent to Coventry, of being ridiculed and humiliated. Many children were haunted by fear—fear of parental disapproval, fear of an early death (all too common in all classes), fear of Hell as vividly depicted by preachers and sometimes by nurserymaids to compel obedience. Of course, many children did enjoy security and love in their early life but modern ideas that children should be treated as equals and allowed, indeed encouraged, to express themselves freely would have astonished most Victorians. To them— and to the children—naughtiness was sin, not self-expression!

Hippolyte Taine, a Frenchman who visited Britain in the 1860s, noted of the middle classes:

It is obvious to me that, for them, happiness consists in that state: home at six in the evening, an agreeable, faithful wife, tea, four or five children clambering over their knees, and respectful servants.[19]

The virtuous family life, as exemplified by the Royal Family, was indeed the ideal, established by the 1840s and emphasized increasingly there-after. This is the picture that has come down to us of the Victorian middle classes—the close-knit family unit as the foundation of society, to be defended at all costs. The family depended entirely upon the father who was the sole earner—thus a family could be ruined by the untimely death of its head. His word was law to wife, children and servants. He had complete economic control and wide legal powers over his family. On marriage, he obtained possession of his wife's money and retained it if she died. The rules of behaviour were strict, and pressure to conform to the social conventions was constant. This created tensions, so that the picture of cosy contentment in the circle round the fire was not always the true one.

Servants relieved the middle-class wife of housekeeping chores, leaving her with only supervisory duties and time on her hands. During her frequent pregnancies she would withdraw from the social round, as a diary entry for Good Friday 1839 indicates:

> *I am happy in being able to go to church every morning this week. The last three years I have been prevented by being on the sofa at the time.*[20]

At other times she would fill her day with paying and receiving calls (all according to strict rules of etiquette), shopping, and planning her dinner parties. She and her daughters might practise such accomplishments as they had—sketching, piano playing, embroidery. Such a life must have been utterly boring to many women who would echo the thoughts confided to her diary by the 31-year-old Florence Nightingale:

> *O weary days—oh evenings that never seem to end—for how many years have I watched that drawing room clock and thought it would never reach ten! and for twenty, thirty years more to do this! . . . I know nothing like the petty, grinding tyranny of a good English family. And the only alleviation is that the tyrannized submits with a heart full of affection.*[21]

Not many women had the strength of will of Miss Nightingale—or Elizabeth Barrett—to break free. Young girls, utterly dependent on their father, found marriage the only socially acceptable goal. The married woman, indeed, was a chattel of her husband—divorce, expensive, difficult to obtain and leading to social ruin, only became possible in England in 1857. But the unmarried woman remained a dependant, without even the status of mistress of the household.

Young men who (like Anthony Trollope) found themselves unable to afford marriage until their income improved (Trollope's salary as a clerk in the Post Office in the 1830s began at £90 a year, on which he became *hopelessly in debt*) might take their sexual pleasures with girls of the servant or working class.

> *Seduction of girls (from the lower orders) is a sport and a habit with vast numbers of men, married . . . and single, placed above the ranks of labour.*[22]

In fact, behind the facade of secure mid-Victorian family life lurked the underworld of prostitution, on a much greater scale than today. In face of the threat it posed, polite society steadfastly ignored its existence, while tacitly allowing it to continue. Thus another element emerges in the relationship between the classes.

[1]*Lords' Select Committee*, 1863; [2]the *Edinburgh Review*, April 1862; [3]*Plenty and Want* by John Burnett (PENGUIN, 1968); [4]*English Notebooks* by Nathaniel Hawthorne, ed. by R. Stewart (RUSSELL & RUSSELL, N.Y., 1962); [5a]*Shops and Shopping* by Alison Adburgham (ALLEN & UNWIN, 1964); [5b]from *Jane Carlyle: A New Selection of her Letters* ed. by Trudy Bliss, quoted in Adburgham, op. cit.; [6]*Prosperity and Parenthood* by J. A. Banks (ROUTLEDGE & KEGAN PAUL, 1954); [7]*The Shops and Companies of London and the Trades and Manufactories of Great Britain* by Henry Mayhew, quoted in *Death, Heaven and the Victorians* by John Morley (STUDIO VISTA, 1971); [8a]from Gorhambury MSS: Monson MSS, 25/10/3/2, No. 32, quoted in *English Landed Society in the Nineteenth Century* by F. M. L. Thompson (ROUTLEDGE & KEGAN PAUL, 1971); [8b]Thompson, op. cit.; [9]from *Frazer's*, Vol. XXXVII, quoted in *Victorian Working Women* by W. F. Neff (FRANK CASS, 1966); [10]*The Life of Charlotte Bronte* by Elizabeth Gaskell (PENGUIN, 1975); [11]*The Life of H.R.H. The Prince Consort*, Vol. II by Sir Theodore Martin, 1874; [12]*Divine Songs* by Isaac Watts (OXFORD UNIV. PRESS, 1971); [13]from *Alton Locke* by Charles Kingsley, quoted in *Victoria and the Victorians* by H. Tingsten (DELACORTE, N.Y., 1972); [14]*Emma* by Jane Austen (PENGUIN, 1970); [15]*Jane Austen's Letters* ed. by R. W. Chapman (OXFORD UNIV. PRESS, 1955); [16]*Modern Cookery for Private Families* by Eliza Acton (ELEK, 1966); [17]*The Book of Household Management* by Mrs Beeton (CAPE, 1968); [18]from *The Modern Housewife* by Alexis Soyer, quoted in *The Early Victorians* by J. F. C. Harrison (WEIDENFELD & NICOLSON, 1971); [19]*Notes on England* by Hippolyte Taine (BOOKS FOR LIBRARIES, INC., N.Y., 1957); [20]from *Dulce Domum* by C. A. E. Moberly, quoted in *Their First Ten Years* by M. Lochhead (JOHN MURRAY, 1956); [21]*Florence Nightingale* by C. Woodham-Smith (PENGUIN, 1953); [22]*Prostitution* by William Acton (FRANK CASS, 1972).

2. Working Classes

When the term "working class" is used now, we tend to think of urban industrial workers. In 1837, however, more than half the working population was still employed in tasks connected with agriculture. This was probably the poorest section of the working class and those living in the South and East of England were in especially bad circumstances.

Before the Agrarian Revolution the peasant could graze livestock on the common, had at least a garden around his cottage, and sometimes a piece of land for farming, could gather wood for building and fuel, and supplemented his income from outwork such as cloth-making or lace manufacture.

By 1837, things had changed. The common and woodlands had been enclosed, and the labourer was lucky if he still had a garden. Outwork was diminishing, so most of his additional income had vanished; agricultural machinery was beginning to reduce the labour needed on farms. Only specialists were employed by the year, while labourers were hired by the day, and were therefore unemployed for long periods.

The Speenhamland System, introduced to assist such men, had created so many problems that the new Poor Law was substituted. By the beginning of Victoria's reign, the effects of this legislation were becoming apparent. Wages had not risen as expected, and were in fact beginning to drop. This was a process which was to continue. Eventually wages in the South and East of England dropped to 6s. per week when a man was fully employed. But this seldom happened, and even one day's work per week disqualified a man from receiving any kind of poor relief.

Housing was also affected by the 1834 Act. A qualification for obtaining poor relief was that the applicant should have been resident in that parish for five years. Increasingly a farmer would only allow a man to settle in a house for four years. At the end of that time he was evicted so that he would never become a charge on the parish. Some landowners took the matter a stage farther and either demolished houses or allowed them to decay. A few houses might be built for specialists, such as carters, stockmen or shepherds, but the labourers were driven out of these "closed" villages and had to live up to four miles away in "open" villages, whose houses with their thin, damp walls and unstable foundations soon became slums, the ownership of which barred the inhabitants from poor relief. This was a situation which became worse and led to such discontent that rural arson became a common crime.

A description of a labourer's cottage was given in the *Morning Chronicle* in 1850:

> *The length is not above 15 feet, its width between 10 and 12. The wall . . . has sunk at different parts, and seems bedewed with a cold sweat. . . . You have to stoop for admission . . . there are but two rooms in the house—one below and the other above. . . . Before you is a large but cheerless fireplace . . . with a few smouldering embers of a small wood fire, over which hangs a pot. . . . At one corner stands a small rickety table, whilst scattered about are three old chairs . . . and a stool or two. . . . Let us take a glance at their sleeping accommodation. . . . There is but one room, and yet we counted nine in the family! . . . The beds are large sacks, filled with chaff of oats. . . . It not infrequently happens that the clothes worn by the parents in the daytime form the chief part of the covering of the children by night. . . .[1]*

Information from other areas in South and East England suggests that this was not an outstanding case. Indeed in some areas the overcrowding was even worse.

It was only in the North, previously the "poor" area, that farm workers had improved their circumstances. The main reason for this was proximity to the new industries. If farmers wanted workers then they had to pay them well enough to fight off the counter-attractions of the towns. Houses were newer, larger and of better quality than in the South. Wages were usually paid partially in kind; for example, one man was paid 36 bushels of oats, 24 of barley, 12 of peas, 3 of wheat, 3 of rye, 40 of potatoes, 24 lbs of wool, £4 in cash, and given a free cottage and garden, coal, and maintenance for a cow each year. Most workers there seemed content with conditions.

The rural poor in the South were badly fed. Potatoes and bread, with bacon on Sundays seem to have been the staple diet, with water the only beverage. In those families where the father did drink beer it is clear that it must have been at the expense of his children.

Even to the contemporary observer,

the means by which he [the farm labourer] obtains his clothes is admitted
by almost everyone to be a mystery!

It would seem that for many, a change of clothing was an unobtainable
luxury. Children were often without shoes, and garments were described
as being *"of rag and patchwork!"*.

Inevitably the health of rural workers was not good under
these conditions. The long hours either working or looking for work
took their toll. Rheumatism was especially common, and in Eastern
England was eased by liberal doses of opium. In the event of ill health
there was only the workhouse to fall back on and in some areas even
gaining admittance was a problem since the guardians were concerned
to keep the poor rate as low as possible.

By 1850 the effects of this situation were such that a reporter
wrote:

It is one of the anomalies of the Poor Law that the pauper is better fed,
better clothed and better lodged than the labourer.[1]

Increasingly, the only way a labourer's child was likely to receive an
education was if his family entered the workhouse. Many farmers
regarded education as an unnecessary luxury for their own children and
were infuriated that money should be spent on educating paupers.

The case of the Tolpuddle Martyrs had emphasized to the
rural working class how much they were under the eye of authority and
how well authority could use the law against them. The harsh administration of the Game Law was another example of this. But the scattered
nature of the rural work force and the small insular villages made it
difficult for radical organizations to operate without knowledge of this
reaching employers. In this especially, the rural worker was worse off
than his urban counterpart.

The problem which confronts us when we try to gauge the
condition of the urban working class in Victorian Britain is that their
situation could change so rapidly. Mrs C. S. Peel has summed this up by
asking:

Do you mean the man in good work with a garden, with the loaf at 7d;
or the same man a few months later in a slum cellar, out of work with the
loaf at 1s?[2]

The top 15% of the working class, comprising male factory
workers and skilled men in traditional trades, were well paid, and more
important, had fairly regular employment But for most, the Industrial
Revolution had brought greater poverty and insecurity. This was to

The family shown in James Collinson's *Answering the Emigrant's Letter* is obviously not of the poorest class—skilled working-class perhaps? At least one child can write. By the mid-1850s, over 150,000 people were leaving Britain each year, mainly for North America.

remain the case until after 1851. The repeal of the Elizabethan Statute of Articifers in 1814 had ended apprenticeship, and by 1837 this had resulted in the numerous unskilled workers reducing the status of the skilled men in many trades.

Many were already looking back to the "good old days" of 1814 when a handloom weaver could earn 34s. 6d., compared to 12s. 6d. in 1838, and these earnings would drop to 4s. 6d. per week in a few more years. For those like handloom and silk weavers, mechanization meant the destruction of their lives. What had seemed a secure trade could no longer provide a bare living and no compensation or retraining was then provided. Their position was not helped by the new Poor Law nor by the middle-class belief in self-help.

The nineteenth-century urban worker was more vulnerable than the eighteenth-century agricultural worker had been. During industrial depressions he had no field work to fall back on, nor was casual work available, since all industries tended to be depressed simultaneously.

Work differed greatly in urban areas. In Yorkshire and Lancashire it was more plentiful than in other regions but overproduction

17

could cause gluts, and massive unemployment resulted. Few industries were fully mechanized and outwork was often available around mill towns, but this was always the first area to suffer during depressions. Even in good times men looked back to the freedom of the domestic system, when they worked when they pleased, in preference to the factory discipline. Work too was faster, noisier and more boring than before.

The 1833 Factory Act left adult workers dissatisfied since it had not limited their hours, while the restrictions it placed on children often broke up the family as a working unit. Owners introduced a shift system for children which lengthened the working day for adults to sixteen hours, and left children unsupervised by their parents for half the working day.

London had been largely by-passed by industrialization because of the high rents and the cost of coal. Nonetheless, the influx of people to the capital was as great as that to the industrial towns. These joined the many partially-employed Londoners who tried to scrape a living in casual work. Many women became involved in tailoring which had a brisk season when Society demanded new dresses at a day's notice but which was stagnant for long periods. The "honourable" or union members in all London trades earned good money and were usually regarded as being the best tradesmen in the country, but they were few in number, and decreased every year under the pressure of the "dishonourable" or "slop" trade, in which large numbers of unskilled or semi-skilled workers scrambled for the limited amount of work available, and accepted steadily decreasing payment, as Mayhew described in his articles.

Investigation into working-class housing about 1837 is hampered by two contradictory facts. The first, that reporters

> described the worst of what they knew, either from a wish to shock the public into reform or from the journalist's wish to tell a dramatic story.

The second is that a house *actually surviving from the period* is *a sample selected by time, almost certainly better than the average for its period or it would not have survived.*[3]

Given these warnings, however, there is a great deal of evidence as to how bad and how good housing could be during this period. Chadwick's *Report on the Sanitary Conditions of the Labouring Population of Great Britain* in 1842 supplies much of this, but some can also be found in doctors' reports and from house plans.

For the first time, class was beginning to determine where a family lived and the result of this was noted by Chadwick:

Urban overcrowding: a one-room family.

The statements of the conditions of considerable proportions of the labouring population . . . have been received with surprise by persons of the wealthier classes living in the immediate vicinity, to whom the facts were as strange as if related to foreigners or the natives of an unknown country.[4a]

Shortage of land in town centres led to the sub-division of larger houses, with a family and often a lodger in each room. Even cellars were used for living space. Gardens were built over and, especially in Yorkshire, inn yards became sites for unventilated back-to-back houses which became immediate slums because of lack of planning and poor building materials.

These properties were "desirable" to landlords only. Single rooms were let for from 1s. 6d. to 3s. per week. These high rents were justified by the claim that insolvent tenants often left without paying rent.

Housekeeping was of a low standard but

> . . . *when slum-dwellers were criticized for failing to keep their houses clean*

it was often forgotten that many had been born and brought up in the country,

> *in conditions where scrubbing was not a possibility*[3]

because of the earthen floors.

Another problem was the shortage of water. At best, a well was available in most towns, but often no addition had been made to the water supply, although the population might have increased four-fold. In Jacob's Island in London, Beames found that a stagnant ditch which surrounded the area and into which the waste from tanneries and glue factories drained was

> *the common sewer of the neighbourhood and the only source from which the wretched inhabitants can get the water which they drink—with which they wash—and with which they cook their victuals.*[5]

When water had to be carried for some distance or had to be bought, few people used it generously in washing either themselves or their clothes.

The exteriors of these "Rookeries" were, if anything, even worse than their interiors. In the middle of most squares of houses were found middens in which all the refuse of the surrounding houses collected. Usually this was because local authorities did not have a collection service, but in some towns such as Glasgow, these midden heaps were jealously guarded since the contents were sold once a year to farmers for manure. Horses, cows, pigs and slaughterhouses added to the appalling urban smells.

It may seem surprising that anyone stayed in such accommodation, but at that time people *had* to live within walking distance of their work. This was especially true of casual workers who had to live close to possible work. Housing shortages in industrial areas led to high rents and allowed landlords to refuse to do more than essential repairs. Food too was cheaper in slum areas and since employment was sporadic, most families found it advisable to stay in areas where they were known, since it was then easier for them to obtain credit.

Not all towns in Britain had such poor housing. In Nottingham, some of the better-paid craftsmen had comfortable and well-furnished homes, and in new towns, to which a working population had to be attracted, employers built good solid houses which they let at a reasonable rent to their workers. This meant that the employer had greater control over his men. Mechanics' Institutes were built rather than public houses, to encourage people to spend their time profitably and soberly. In one village, Saddleworth, in Yorkshire, five-apartment houses were let for 3s. 1d. per week, and for an additional 6d. tenants could have gas lighting, which they could

> keep alight until half-past ten, and on Saturdays and Sundays as long as they pleased.[1]

Health was of course closely linked with housing conditions. When we read in Beames that some London houses had seventy-two inhabitants in six rooms, it is easy to see why diseases spread so quickly. The first great epidemic of cholera in 1831–32 had caused panic among the urban population of Britain. It is worth noting that the Government had foreknowledge of its effects on the Continent, and suggested that ships from infected ports should not land cargoes in Britain. This was ignored, since port authorities preferred to risk the nation's health rather than their own profits. It was this type of government which led to Carlyle's description of "laissez-faire" as

> abdication on the part of the governors.[4b]

Governments of that time did not know how to handle the health problems which resulted from the rapid growth of towns. Statistics were already indicating how unhealthy town life was for the working class. In Liverpool, for example, average life expectancy for the middle classes was 35 years, that of the working classes, 15 years. The 62% mortality of working-class children largely accounted for this, but adulterated food and water supplies also contributed. Young children who had no place to play but the streets with their stagnant puddles, or back courts with their midden heaps, were very vulnerable to infection, and the cost of doctors as well as their lack of medical knowledge meant there was little chance of survival.

Even after death a body could remain as a source of infection to the rest of the family. When a family lived in a single room, the corpse had to remain there until the funeral took place, and life continued around it. Working-class funerals took place on a Sunday, to avoid a day's absence from work. Postponements till the following week, until money had been collected for the funeral payment, often happened. Chadwick mentions that in some areas, "women of the lowest class" were sometimes heard to comment:

> Aye, aye, that child will not live; it is in the burial club;[6]

implying that the parents would profit from the child's death.

Accidents and heavy factory work also contributed to ill health and deformity, so that by the end of the 1830s, the health situation in towns was causing concern. The second generation of urban dwellers was noticeably less healthy, and this, as well as the epidemics which to some extent affected the wealthier in towns, led to an investigation of conditions in major towns. This was the first step and Civil Servants like Chadwick were the people who maintained pressure for action, although lack of knowledge about sewerage and medicine was an obstacle.

Diet, food supply and income were also linked with poor health. Population expansion was never equalled by food consumption. Although the population of London doubled between 1801 and 1841, beef supplies went up only one and a half times and the same was true of other commodities. When women were working, cooking was impossible and in any case most houses had only a fireplace and no stove. Those families who could afford it sent meat to the baker to be cooked, but most ate mainly bread or bought potatoes or pies from street vendors. The working class usually bought food supplies in the most expensive way—in small quantities. Lack of storage utensils meant buying twists of tea and sugar every time tea was made, and in any case money was not available for bulk buying. Following fashion led most of the working class to buy more expensive, but often less nutritious, food. White bread, for example, was positively harmful because of the addition of alum, and dearer than the "inferior" whole-wheat.

In the same way, the working class copied the wealthier in their dress. In 1871 Blanchard Jerrold was to write:

> An English crowd is almost the ugliest in the world: because the poorer classes are but copyists in costume of the rich.[7]

A more likely explanation is that the poor did not have money to buy new clothes and the result was second-hand ones which had made their way down the social scale. Money was too short for much to go on clothing, and certainly a change of clothing was almost unknown. Indeed in some houses in Glasgow, so far from people having a second outfit, there was sometimes only one set between two people, where some tenants worked during the day and others at night. Those not at work had to stay in bed. Shoes too were a luxury, especially for children, most of whom went barefoot at least in summer.

Education was as yet of little importance to most of the working class, although the relaxation of the Stamp Duty on newspapers in 1832 had given a greater incentive to literacy. Some children did have

THE USE OF ADULTERATION.

Little Girl. "IF YOU PLEASE, SIR, MOTHER SAYS, WILL YOU LET HER HAVE A QUARTER OF A POUND OF YOUR BEST TEA TO KILL THE RATS WITH, AND A OUNCE OF CHOCOLATE AS WOULD GET RID OF THE BLACK BEADLES?"

THE MAIN QUESTION.

Girl. "ANY USE OF ME WAITING?"
Boy. "NO; I ONLY CAME YESTERDAY MORNING, AND AIN'T HALF FULL YET."

the two hours schooling which the 1833 Act demanded, but as most employers valued cheapness more than training in teachers the children did not receive much benefit. Most of them were in any case too tired to learn much. Statistics about literacy are confusing and depend on whether an ability to write one's name was sufficient or whether something more was demanded. One set of figures for 1837 states that 40% of men and 65% of women were illiterate. Attendance at school did not guarantee learning. Dames' schools were generally child-minding institutions and many of the charity schools had masters who were appointed through nepotism. Mechanics' Institutes were mainly patronized by the middle classes but some working men did attend, and improved their position in life as a result.

Yet education was expanding at this time because of the money available through the Education Grant, and the appointment of Government Inspectors was leading to improved standards. Sunday Schools made some contribution too, although the original intention was to prevent youths lounging around streets on Sundays. We must have some sympathy for those who decided on relaxation rather than self-improvement after their long hours of work.

Ragged Schools were another area of voluntary effort. Undoubtedly these too were founded with the best of motives but the contemporary descriptions suggest thieves' schools rather than academic ones. One horrified visitor found the pupils departing at eight o'clock lest they miss the best time for pick-pocketing.

In Scotland the situation was different. Since 1694 the Church of Scotland had insisted that there be a school in every parish, and most people, in the Lowlands at least, were literate. Secondary schools existed in all burghs. In Glasgow it was even possible for a working man to attend university at night, thanks to the efforts of Professor Anderson, and many acquired a degree in this way during the nineteenth century.

At that time it was mainly with the middle classes that the working classes came into conflict in the towns. In 1849 one of the *Morning Chronicle*'s journalists wrote:

Capital and labour look at each other with suspicious eyes. The owner of the former characterizes the owner of the latter as one of the "dangerous classes"—only perhaps to be characterized in his turn as one of the "tyrannous classes".[1]

Many of the working class believed that
the principle of supply and demand has been extended from commodities to men,[8]
and resented the resulting loss of individuality. The new middle class

often expected from the working class the deference and respect which had hitherto been shown only to the upper class. The middle-class motto:

What some men are, all without difficulty might be,[9]

seemed to the working class to imply that they were without energy or self-control, and they answered with the argument that

regularity of habits are incompatible with irregularity of income.[1]

So bitter did the clash become that some of the working class believed that cholera had been deliberately introduced in 1832 by the middle classes to reduce the numbers of the poor.

Those of the working class who were determined to improve not just their own position but that of their fellow workers too, were by 1837 trying to develop some means of exerting working-class influence. They were decided on the need to work out their own salvation in this matter. They had not forgotten the events of 1832 when the working class had exerted pressure on the Government and the middle class had reaped the reward. In future they would work out their own destiny and avoid being manipulated for the benefit of others.

[1]*The Victorian Working Class* ed. by P. E. Razzell and R. W. Wainwright (FRANK CASS, 1973); [2]from *Homes and Habits* by Mrs C. S. Peel, quoted in *Early Victorian England 1830–1865* ed. by G. M. Young (OXFORD UNIV. PRESS, 1934); [3]*Cruel Habitations* by Enid Gauldie (ALLEN & UNWIN, 1974); [4a]from Chadwick's *Report on the Sanitary Condition of the Labouring Population of Great Britain*, 1842, quoted in *Origins of Modern English Society 1780–1880* by H. Perkin (ROUTLEDGE & KEGAN PAUL, 1972); [4b]Perkin, op. cit.; [5]*The Rookeries of London* by T. Beames (FRANK CASS, 1970); [6]from Chadwick's *Supplementary Report on the Results of a Special Inquiry into the Practice of Interment in Towns*, Vol. XII, 1843, quoted in *Human Documents of the Industrial Revolution* by E. Royston Pike (ALLEN & UNWIN, 1967); [7]*London: A Pilgrimage* by Gustave Doré and Blanchard Jerrold (DAVID & CHARLES, 1971); [8]from *Lectures on Social Sciences and Organization of Labour* by J. Hole, 1851, quoted in *Victorian Cities* by Asa Briggs (PENGUIN, 1968); [9]*Self-Help* by Samuel Smiles (SPHERE, 1970).

Part Two
Responses

1. Working Classes

Trade unions, often continuations of the Craft Guilds, were commented on by Adam Smith:

The workmen desire to get as much, the masters to give as little as possible. The former are disposed to combine in order to raise, the latter in order to lower, the wages of labour.[1]

John Rennie, the engineer, found

... a particular class of skilled workmen embodied into a special Guild or Craft for making machinery, and they would not ... admit any man to work with them unless they (sic) had been apprenticed for the same number of years to a master millwright as themselves....[2a]

Despite the Combination Laws, these unions continued to exist, usually disguised as friendly societies but also protecting the status of their members against the unskilled and unemployed who, in desperation, would "blackleg" by accepting lower wages. This led some to see unions as *"monopolies of skilled against unskilled workers"*.

Some of their methods were extreme. In the trial of seven Glasgow cotton spinners in 1838, evidence was given that

the guards' [pickets'] duty was to try to take out the new hands who were working at reduced rates, and to prevent others going in. The means were— by advising, treating to drink, or assaulting.[3]

Another witness spoke of

a sort of bomb thrown into a manufacturer's house and a cotton worker struck with combustibles,[3]

and ended ominously:

On Sunday, heard officially of Smith's murder[3]

for which the prosecution alleged the union had paid.

The workmen involved in this kind of activity were usually those whose skill was quickly acquired, since this made it difficult to prevent wages from falling. They provided most of the members of Owen's Grand National Consolidated Trade Union, hoping to obtain support from this mass movement and what they hoped would be its

"The Blackleg"

mass finances. Owen, on the other hand, had wanted his union to change society from competition into co-operation.

After its collapse, many workers found they could only obtain work if they signed the Document, promising not to join a union. This was used by employers until the 1850s, when workmen declared their promise no longer binding since it was given under duress.

By 1838, it was true to say that only those who were very skilled in their trade, or were members of an elite trade, belonged to unions. While investigating the conditions of furniture workers in London, Mayhew noticed the marked difference

. . . between the abode of the workmen in a good West-end establishment, and the garret or cellar of the toiler for a "slaughter-house" at the East-end. In the one you have the warm red glow of polished mahogany furniture; a clean carpet covers the floor; a few engravings in neat frames hang against the papered wall; and bookshelves or a bookcase have their appropriate furniture. Very white and bright coloured pot ornaments, with sometimes a few roses in a small vase, are reflected in a mirror over the mantel-shelf.

C

The East-end cabinet-maker's room has one *piece of furniture, which is generally the principal—the workman's bench. The walls are bare and sometimes the half-black plaster is crumbling from them; all is dark and dingy, and of furniture there is very little, and that, it must be borne in mind, when the occupant is a furniture-maker.*[4]

Trade unions still found it necessary to safeguard themselves against spies from employers and the Government. The Order of Friendly Boiler Makers, which was formed in 1834, began its initiation by having the new member repeat the following vow:

I . . . do most solemnly declare and promise, before God and this assembly, that I will keep inviolable all the secrets or transactions that I do hear, see or receive, relative tō this order, namely;—"The Order of Friendly Boiler Makers", especially the grip, words, signs, or countersigns of a Friendly Boiler Maker, except it be unto a Friendly Boiler Maker, whom I believe to be a true and Friendly brother amongst us, and that I will be true and steadfast in all things lawful and not otherwise. . . .[5]

Most workmen did not have the skills or money necessary to join a union, and to them the political activity of the Chartists seemed most likely to bring relief from hardships. Most of the six points of the People's Charter were discussed long before 1838 when the Charter was first published. Previously, middle-class radical reform groups had produced these ideas. Lovett, in founding the London Working Men's Association, had as his aim the regeneration of the working classes through education into political awareness.

Although several of the Chartist leaders, such as O'Connor, were middle-class, most Chartists saw it as

a movement of the working classes[6]

and were wary of approaches from other reform groups. Those who had demonstrated in 1832 in favour of the Reform Bill, believed that subsequent legislation had been of benefit to the middle classes only. One of those, disillusioned by the "Sham Radicals" of 1832, said in 1837:

Your Whig is dressed in hen's feathers and has a sheep's heart in his bosom. . . . Your Tory is a straight-forward robber and cut-throat. . . .[6]

It was from the mixture of Lovett's idealism and these suspicions that Chartism came into being.

Chartists were not always the

honest, sober and reflecting portion of every town and village in the kingdom[7a]

that Lovett had hoped for. Some of these joined and were sometimes prominent in the movement, but most Chartists were rather those who were losing status in the new industrial society, especially handloom weavers, and those who were insecure—for example, those who lived in a single industry town. Those who were normally secure, such as skilled workers in their trade unions, only gave support to the Chartists in times of great depression, and usually dropped out when trade conditions improved. Their lack of support was a cause of bitterness to Chartist leaders, one of whom referred to this group as

the pompous trades and proud mechanics.[8]

From the beginning, Chartism was split between Lovett's moral force ideals and O'Connor's verbal support of physical force. Lovett's declaration:

Whatever is gained in England by force, by force must be sustained; but whatever springs from knowledge and justice will sustain itself[9a]

was countered by those who adopted a more violent approach, such as the Chartist in Newcastle who said in 1839:

Parliament does not represent me and I will not obey its laws.[6]

The prosperity of an area was the main factor in whether it would opt for physical or moral force. As one Chartist leader, quoted in the *Northern Liberator* of 28 December 1838, said of moderates:

These men were well-fed and therefore relied on moral force; but let them labour for one week and be ill-fed and ill-clothed and it would soon convert their moral force to physical force.[10]

The industrial area of Scotland which was then benefiting from the growth of the iron industry was thus a moral force region, while the North of England and Wales supported physical force.

The actual pressure that the moral force supporters could bring to bear was always a matter of dispute, but in 1839 a list of suggestions was drawn up for discussion at Chartist meetings. Among other points, the list included supporting a run on banks, a national strike, a boycott of rents, rates and taxes, exclusive dealing in shops owned by Chartists, and obeying "laws" passed by the Chartist Convention. But even these moral force Chartists asked

whether according to their old constitutional right, they have prepared themselves with the arms of free men to defend the laws and constitutional privileges their ancestors bequeathed to them.[11a]

The tactic of exclusive dealing had already been successfully pioneered at Oldham during the 1832 election, when it had resulted in 100 out of 109 grocers and all 49 publicans voting for the Radical candidates, but when various Chartist groups tried it, they found on the whole what the Oldham workers had already discovered, namely that the better-off section of the town could use their superior buying power to counteract this device. O'Connor was never in favour of the sacred month, and gave his reasons for this in the *Northern Star*:

If I thought you could test the value of labour by a month's holiday, I would say have it. . . . But you know—you all know—that the baker will not bake, the butcher will not kill, and the brewer will not brew; and then what becomes of the millions of starving human beings? . . . Make your necessary arrangements; have a three days' holiday, instead of a month's strike, and what you fail to effect by it, would have been equally lost by the month . . . but I never will, with a certainty of my own dinner, recommend a project which may cause millions to starve. . . .[11b]

The three days' strike was substituted but the problem of the moral force Chartists was underlined. Before the presentation of the first petition to Parliament, the question had been:

How are the people to obtain the Charter, there being a majority of the Commons against it?[6]

and with even greater despair:

What shall we do if the Charter is refused?[6]

After the refusal, one Chartist described moral force as

trying to drive a nail with a feather[6]

and more began to adopt the motto:

Peacefully if we may, forcibly if we must.[6]

O'Connor had already pointed out:

They might depend upon it, however, that the moment moral force failed, physical force would slip in. . . .[11c]

How far O'Connor was prepared to take part in any physical fighting is a matter for debate, but certainly both he and his closest supporters did make speeches and write articles which were aimed not only at discrediting the moral force side of the movement but at inciting violence. He sneered at Lovett's plans for educating the "intelligent minds", saying:

In fact, it is nothing more or less than a new mode of canvassing support for the Mechanics' Institutes. . . .[11d]

There is no clear information about the existence of a Chartist uprising. It does seem that those who rose with Frost at Newport were expecting support from other parts of the country, and in many areas Chartists were armed. A letter from the *Northern Star* in March 1839 read:

There is not a labouring man here from 16 to 60, who has not signed the petition and there is a pike for every signature.[11e]

Pamphlets exhorted the readers to

be ready then to nourish the tree of liberty WITH THE BLOOD OF TYRANTS.[11f]

The trial of Holberry at Sheffield in 1840 heard evidence that police found guns, bullets, daggers and primitive hand-grenades in a Chartist's house. Chartists claimed they only armed because they feared the Government would attack them, but the arms reported found by the police and the plans which seem to have been current in some areas suggest that some Chartists were prepared to rise in arms to achieve their objective.

The problem of being verbally inflammatory but yet staying on the right side of the law was not the only one which O'Connor had to face. Increasingly, other ideas and objectives appealed to Chartists of various areas. In some it was Christian Chartism, and from one of their services came the following prayer:

Almighty God! ... We confess before Thee with shame and confusion that we have sinned against Thee—and that we have broken Thy most holy laws, and that in the payment of rates for the support of the Established Church, which is opposed to Thee both in word and deed....

King of kings! and Lord of lords! have mercy on the Queen, shew unto her the error of her ways ... convince her that she cannot be the mother of her country whilst so many of her children are starving for lack of food— that she receives too much money for merely living in a large house, and signing acts of Parliament, for oppressing the people, Thy servants. Oh Lord, convert her and her Royal husband....

And now, oh Lord! May we depart in peace. Direct the Council of the people now sitting in a distant part of the country—may the means they may resort to be consistent with the glory, and further emancipation of Thy servants. Bless our enemies—convert the lawyers,—the spies,—the soldiers,—the police, and all others that have been engaged in the unjust persecution of the people; and to Thy name, Oh Parent of mankind, shall be the glory.[7b]

It is easy to see why so many Chartists sought their own place of worship when we read of a vicar taking as the text for his working-class congregation:

I have learned, in whatever station of life, therewith to be content.[6]

Another off-shoot of Chartism was teetotalism. The drunkenness of certain sections of the working class aroused as great condemnation from Lovett and Vincent in particular as did the oppression of the upper classes. Edinburgh Chartists reported in 1844:

The most chilling, the most heart-rending view that meets our sight is on a Saturday night, when we leave our deliberations, ... and behold the hundreds, issuing from the pothouses in a state degrading to themselves, and revolting to humanity.[6]

It was this section of the public which roused Vincent to write:

The lower stratum of the working classes has no political past—or future.[6]

Teetotalism was also a way in which pressure could be brought to bear on the Government, since duties on alcohol contributed substantially to the national income. This was probably why Robert Cranston of Edinburgh was charged with

preaching sedition under the guise of temperance.[6]

These were some of the internal pressures which tended to divide the Chartist movement. O'Connor was always bitterly hostile to those who became side-tracked on what he called

the Religious, Knowledge and Temperance Chartism HUMBUG.[6]

He maintained:

If Chartists you are, Chartists remain; you have enough work without entering into the new maze prepared for you. . . . Get your Charter, and I will answer for the religion, sobriety, knowledge, and house, and a bit of land into the bargain. . . .[6]

Similar bodies to the Chartists also contended for working-class support. One of these was the Birmingham Political Union which had a very similar reform programme, but which had some middle-class members, who dominated it and held the posts of importance. This was unacceptable to working-class Chartists, and although for a while the B.P.U. had branches and support in many areas these soon died out.

The Complete Suffrage Union was another such body but again the working class and O'Connor were suspicious of it. A meeting for combined action was held in Birmingham in 1842 but ended in a split between the two groups because of the refusal of the C.S.U. to adopt the name Chartist even although it was willing to support the programme.

With the Anti-Corn Law League and the Ten Hour Movement this same problem came to the forefront. Certainly the working classes would benefit by the success of these but the leadership was in the hands of members of the wealthier classes, and the Chartists were suspicious of both them and their motives.

The challenge from the A.C.L.L. was especially strong and their programme one which appealed to many members of the working classes who could see the immediate advantages it was likely to bring them. Their view was succinctly put by the man who said he was

for the Charter, but not for being starved first.[6]

For this reason the Chartists had to be especially strong in their response. In 1840 one Chartist spokesman put their point of view:

Not that the Corn Law Repeal is wrong; when we get the Charter we will
repeal the Corn Laws and all other bad laws. But if you give up your
agitation for the Charter to help the Free Traders, they will not help you
get the Charter. Don't be deceived by the middle classes again. You helped
them get their votes. . . . But where are the fine promises they made you?
Gone to the winds! They said when they had gotten their votes, they would
help you get yours. . . . And now they want to get the Corn Laws repealed
—not for your benefit—but for their own. "Cheap bread" they cry. But
they mean "Low wages". Do not listen to their cant and humbug. Stick to
your Charter. You are veritable slaves without your votes![12]

The other diversions had also to be dealt with.

What is the remedy? the Chartists in Manchester asked. *Trade Unions?*
No, they have been tried and found wanting. Repeal the Poor Law, the
rural police, the Game Law, the money or the Corn Law, or any single law
on the Statute Book and leave the root of the evil untouched, and you will be
only dabbling with the effects of class legislation![6]

By the mid-1840s the Chartist appeal was beginning to fade.
Many had been alienated by the underlying violence of the Chartist
propaganda. Others had drifted off when the economic situation
improved. Some of the younger men who might have provided the
next generation of leaders had found it advisable to emigrate when the
authorities began to take too close an interest in their doings. There
was a resurgence of interest in 1847–48 partly because of the revolutions
on the Continent, partly because of another, but less damaging depression, and partly because rural areas for the first time became interested
in Chartism, because of the Land Scheme. This latter plan soon col-
lapsed, and although the Chartists continued to hold Conventions until
1858, and achieved some success in local government elections during
this time, the support of the earlier days was never regained.

The trade unions during this period were growing, but had
on the whole little connection with Chartism. Individuals might be
members of both, and there were some unions which benefited from
Chartism, such as the Miners' Association which used the *Northern Star*
as a means of communication among members, but on the whole it was
the weaker unions which amalgamated with the Chartists, seeking in
the larger body the strength which they lacked. The Chartists were often
bitter over the failure of the still small but closely-knit craft unions to
give them support. Ernest Jones wrote virulently that

of all aristocracies, the aristocracy of labour has been the most fatal to the
people,[2b]

but, as the unions pointed out,

their Trades Union was illegal enough at present, and they were unpopular
enough with the masters without making them more so.[6]

Indeed, politics and religion were often banned from discussion at trade union meetings.

Apart from 1842, the members of the elite trades were beginning to make progress during the 1840s, in restricting hours and numbers of apprentices. The benefits which they paid were good, and it was only during the worst depressions that funds for these ran out. The secret society element was still present but the skilled unions were by then seeking legal ways of dealing with their grievances, by lobbying Parliament to obtain legal status and the alteration of industrial legislation such as the Master and Servant Act. Lawyers were employed to represent members in court, and to these men, Chartism seemed a distraction. O'Connor was never a favourite with the skilled unions and was in trouble with the Printers' Union for employing too many apprentices on the *Northern Star*.

Throughout the 1840s the number in these skilled unions was not great, probably less than 150,000. But a growing pride was evident. The unionists claimed that if workmen had to make a choice they

considered it a greater honour to be a Trades Unionist[6]

than a full member of the National Charter Association. They were looking for recognition of their skills and legal protection of these, as the preface to the 1845 *Rules of the Journeymen Steam Engine Machine Makers and Millwrights' Friendly Society* shows:

The youth who has the good fortune and inclination for preparing himself as a useful member of society by the study of physic and who studies that profession with success so as to obtain his diploma from the Surgeons' Hall or College of Surgeons, naturally expects, in some measure, that he be entitled to privileges to which the pretending quack can lay no claim; and if in the practice of that useful profession he finds himself injured by such a pretender, he has the power of instituting a course of law against him. Such are the benefits connected with the learned professions. But the mechanic, though he may expend nearly an equal fortune and sacrifice an equal proportion of his life in becoming acquainted with the different branches of useful mechanism, has no law to protect his privileges.[2b]

During this decade then the two main types of working-class organizations had contrasting development. The Chartists, with their mass movement, tried to attract as many as possible to their number. The unions were exclusive. The Chartists were, in theory, centralized, holding regular meetings which discussed the various issues confronting the movement. The unions were still largely autonomous. The unions too sought secrecy rather than publicity from their meetings. Most important of all was the fact that the Chartists had ultimately no control over their membership. When their central body issued a policy statement, they had no means of ensuring obedience from their members. When a trade union found its policy being infringed by a member, he was expelled, and lost the many financial benefits to which his payment of union dues entitled him. In addition he would find difficulty in gaining employment since his former mates would refuse to work with him. As the Chartists came to the end of the decade with a much weakened membership, the unions reached that point ready to move forward to a consolidation of the expansion which had quietly been going on during the 1840s.

The movement towards larger groupings of each trade, one of the major developments of unions during the 1840s, came about not by policy but because of the growth of larger industrial units which forced unions to adopt a similar policy of amalgamation to maintain a bargaining position. These larger groupings are usually known as the "New Model" unions. But apart from their successful amalgamations there was little that was new about them. Their rules were based on those which the smaller unions had drawn up, and the benefits too were on much the same scale. An important innovation was the employment of professional administrators, men who had worked at the trades concerned and who understood the industrial problems involved, but who were able to give their full time to the work and did not fear being blacklisted by employers, as had happened to many of the earlier branch officials.

The Amalgamated Society of Engineers was the first of these unions to emerge in 1851. It is clear that some of the Chartist jibes of selfishness had disturbed the unions, for the preface to their rules says:

Although objections are at times raised to Trade Societies, being associations of monopoly and of trade restrictions, they are nevertheless necessary adjuncts of a state of society which has inculcated feelings of selfishness almost beyond the control of our better nature, for by them only can the members of a trade be made to observe some rules and conform deferentially to many customs which are for the mutual benefit of all its followers.[13a]

The great insecurity of even skilled craftsmen was also shown:

We are willing to admit that, whilst in constant employment our members may be able to obtain all the necessities and perhaps some of the luxuries of life; are perhaps surrounded by many comforts, and congratulate themselves on being so circumstanced; notwithstanding all this, there is a fear always prominent on the mind of him who thinks of the future, that it may not continue, that tomorrow may see him out of employment; his nicely arranged domestic comfort overthrown; and his hopes of being able in a few years by constant attention and frugality, to occupy a more permanent position, proved only to be a dream.[13a]

The most noticeable feature of these new unions was their cautious respectability. To be admitted as a member, a man

must be in good health, have worked five years at the trade, be a good workman, of steady habits, of good moral character, and not more than 45 years of age.[13a]

At least two existing members who knew the applicant well had to guarantee him and after the applicant had paid his "proposition money" (usually about 2s. 6d.) he was investigated by the union. If the majority of members then voted to admit him he paid the other half of his admittance money, and thereafter 1s. per week. The benefits of belonging to a union were certainly worth obtaining, but only the skilled, well-paid men could afford to pay for these. The weekly benefits of the Amalgamated Society of Carpenters and Joiners were:

Donation benefit for 12 weeks, 10s. per week; and for another 12 weeks 6s. For leaving employment satisfactory to branch or executive council, 15s. per week. Tool benefit to any amount of loss . . .; sick benefit for 16 weeks, 12s., and then 6s. so long as his illness continues; funeral benefit, £12 . . .; accident benefit, £100; superannuation benefit for life, if a member 25 years, 8s. per week; if a member 18 years, 7s., if a member 12 years, 5s. The emigration benefit is £6, and there are benevolent grants, according to circumstances, in cases of distress.[13a]

The unions were thus acting as insurance companies for members as well as negotiating payment, hours of work, and limitation of apprentices. They tried to ensure sufficient work existed for their members. For this reason the emigration benefit was paid and a kind of labour exchange was run through the union headquarters so that a surplus of labour in one area could be directed to another in which there was work available. In addition to saving money in the payment of benefits this lessened the chances of an employer reducing wages because of a labour surplus. For the same reason apprentices were usually limited to one for every ten journeymen since:

We maintain the skill and labour of the working man, being his capital, the employer has no right to interfere with it by requiring him to instruct a number of boys, whereby his capital,—namely, his labour—will be greatly deteriorated, and probably destroyed.[13b]

This was successful for those who were members of skilled trades unions, but lowered the position of those who were not members. The

New Model unions did not approve of strikes and had very strict procedures to prevent these from happening. The front of the monthly report of the Amalgamated Society of Carpenters and Joiners stated

> *that in the event of the members of any branch of this society being desirous of soliciting their employers for any new privilege, they must first forward to the council full particulars of the privilege required. The council will immediately consider the same, and if circumstances warrant, grant the application; but should the employers fail to comply with the request made, the branch so applying must again consult as to their future course. And under no circumstances will any branch be allowed to strike without first obtaining the sanction of the council, whether it be for a new privilege or against an encroachment on existing ones.*[8]

The new type of amalgamated union had no intention of wasting their substantial funds. When they did authorize a strike, they did not always win their point, but they did make it clear to the employers that their funds would allow them to hold out long enough to make strikes harmful to the employers. The result was that strikes became less common and negotiation the normal procedure.

The growth of these unions was certainly worrying to many of the upper classes. One employer stated in the 1860s:

> *What we have to be afraid of here is a strike, not a socialist coup.*[14]

During that decade, outbreaks of violence, especially in Sheffield, led to criticism, but the skilled unions were successful in proving to the Royal Commission on Trades Unions in 1867 that they were neither violent nor irresponsible. They were helped in this matter by Thomas Hughes, M.P., and Frederic Harrison, and it was mainly due to them that a favourable view of union activities of the well-organized type was finally taken. There were many who were still hostile to them, and they too produced their evidence to the Royal Commission and in the press. The unions were accused of

> *laying the axe to the root of the national resources*[15a]

and of creating

> *an unnatural deficiency in the supply of labour.*[15b]

With more truth it was claimed that the benefits were designed as

> *a bait to attract, but still more forcibly as a tie to retain members in their allegiance.*[15c]

Probably the essence of the objections was that

> *the vicious principle that the workman owes a duty to his fellow workmen paramount to his obligation to his employer, underlies the whole system of the trade unions.*[15c]

The unions did make headway, however, and their demands for greater legal protection for workers and trade unions were later dealt with as a result of this Commission.

It would seem then that the unions, with their apparently selfish and restricted area of activities, had succeeded where the Chartists, with their more idealistic aims, had failed. The opinion that Chartism was a *series of responses, not a movement*[9b] gives one reason for its failure. But Chartism did leave the working classes with leaders who were experienced and articulate, many of whom played important parts in public life and in working-class causes later in the century. The unions had brought in structure and discipline, and given a successful pattern for the less skilled to follow.

[1]*Trade Unions in the Victorian Age*, Vol. III (GREGG INTERNATIONAL, 1974); [2a]from *John Rennie, 1761–1821* by C. T. Boucher, quoted in *The Skilled Artisans during the Industrial Revolution 1750–1850* by W. Chaloner (HISTORICAL ASSOC., 1969); [2b]Chaloner, op. cit.; [3]from the *Edinburgh Review*, Vol. LXVII, 1838, quoted in *Trade Unions in the Victorian Age*, Vol. II (GREGG INTERNATIONAL, 1974); [4]*The Victorian Working Class* ed. by P. E. Razzell and R. W. Wainwright (FRANK CASS, 1973); [5]*History of the United Society of Boilermakers and Iron and Steel Ship-builders* by D. C. Cummings (P. ROBINSON & CO. LTD., CLAVERING PLACE, NEWCASTLE, 1905); [6]*Chartism and the Chartists* by D. Jones (PENGUIN, 1975); [7a]from the *Address and Rules of the Working Men's Association*, June 1836, quoted in *The Early Chartists* ed. by D. Thomson (MAC-MILLAN, 1971); [7b]from the *Northern Star*, August 1840, quoted in Thomson, op. cit.; [8]*1868—Year of the Unions* by E. Frow and M. Katanka (KATANKA, 1968); [9a]from *William Lovett, 1800–77*, Fabian Tract 199 by L. Barbara Hammond, 1922, quoted in *Chartism* by F. C. Mather (HISTORICAL ASSOC., 1972); [9b]from *Victorian Studies*, Vol. V, March 1962, quoted in Mather, op. cit.; [10]*The Miners' Association—A Trade Union in the Age of the Chartists* by R. Challinor and B. Ripley (LAWRENCE & WISHART, 1968); [11a]from *Charter*, 19 May 1839, quoted in *Class and Conflict in Nineteenth-Century England* by P. Hollis (ROUT-LEDGE & KEGAN PAUL, 1973); [11b]from the *Northern Star*, 3 August 1839, quoted in Hollis, op. cit.; [11c]from the *Northern Star*, 27 April 1839, quoted in Hollis, op. cit.; [11d]from the *Northern Star*, 24 April 1841, quoted in Hollis, op. cit.; [11e]from the *Northern Star*, 23 March 1839, quoted in Hollis, op. cit.; [11f]from *The Life of Sir Charles Napier*, Vol. II, 1857, quoted in Hollis, op. cit.; [12]*Chartist Studies* by Asa Briggs (MAC-MILLAN, 1963); [13a]*Labour's Formative Years* by J. B. Jefferys (LAWRENCE & WISHART, 1948); [13b]from J. Doody's Paper to the T.U.C., 1869, quoted in Jefferys, op. cit; [14]*Rise of an Industrial Society in England* by S. G. Checkland (LONGMAN, 1971); [15a]from *Blackwood's Magazine*, Vol. XXXV, March 1834, quoted in *Trade Unions in the Victorian Age, Introduction* (GREGG INTERNATIONAL, 1974); [15b]from the *Edinburgh Review*, Vol. LIX, 1834, quoted in op. cit.; [15c]from the *Edinburgh Review*, Vol. CXXVI, 1867, quoted in op. cit.

2. Middle Classes

By the 1840s, it was true to say that
*industry now stood side by side with hereditary opulence; the
owner of ten thousand spindles confronted the lord of ten thousand acres;
the one grasping the steam-engine, the other the plough; each surrounded by
an equal number of dependants, and bearing an equal share in the burdens
and dangers of the state. Now the time has arrived when the shadow of an
injustice between such rivals could no longer be endured. . . . Trade shall no
longer pay tribute to the soil. . . .*[1a]

The new industrialists had a genuine belief in the value of their
contribution to society:
The cause of Industry is the cause of humanity. . . .[1b]
*It is a proud feeling to an Englishman to know that the productions of the
thousand busy hands and whirling wheels around him are destined to increase
the comfort, refinement, or splendour of nations, spread far and wide over
the globe. . . .*[1c]

In addition to these somewhat idealized notions, they had
powerful economic motives for urging the removal of the Corn Laws
which to them represented the entrenched privilege of the aristocracy.
The call for repeal, in fact, became the rallying cry of the Radical movement in the late 1830s, appealing to a wider range of support than any
other Radical cause, not excluding the campaign for the Ballot.

But in spite of meetings where
there were at least 4000 operatives present[1d]
and the formation of Anti-Corn Law associations by
the working classes of the more respectable sort,[1e]
and although
*many of the better paid and relatively more educated, including . . . former
Chartists, favoured repeal of the Corn Laws,*[1f]
there was little real support from the working classes. Suspicion of the
League's motives appeared, summed up in verse, in the *Northern
Liberator* of 23 May 1840:

Who are that blustering, canting crew,
Who keep the cheap loaf in our view,
And would from us more profit screw?
                    The League.
Who cry "Repeal the curs'd Corn Law",
‘ *And would their workmen feed with straw,*
That they may filthy lucre paw?
                    The League.
Who wish to gull the working man,
And burk the Charter, if they can,
With their self-aggrandizing plan?

                        The League.[2a]

And two Chartists stated in 1840:

What is our present relation to you as a section of the middle class? It is one of violent opposition. You are the holders of power, participation in which you refuse us; for demanding which you persecute us with a malignity paralleled only by the ruffian Tories. We are therefore surprised that you should ask us to co-operate with you.[3]

Yet in terms of class struggle, the League played a vital part in the contest for power between the middle class and the aristocracy. John Bright, in a speech at Covent Garden on 19 December 1845, believed it to be

a movement of the commercial and industrious classes against the lords and great proprietors of the soil . . .[4]

while Robert Peel himself justified repeal as designed

to terminate a conflict which . . . would soon place in hostile collision great and powerful classes in this country.[2a]

The Anti-Corn Law League's main significance, however, was as

an important milestone in the development of English political institutions.[2a]

Its tactics were in many ways those of a modern pressure group. Lecture tours and mass meetings, some in large London theatres, were organized; huge quantities of literature were distributed, carefully selected according to the interests of the recipients; cash payments were made to newspapers which carried Anti-Corn Law articles, often written under assumed names; *The Economist*, founded in 1843 and not officially an organ of the League, also received support. After initial difficulties, the League became skilled at fund-raising and, from 1842 on, was generally well-supplied financially. Increasing prosperity after 1842 enabled contributors to be generous and methods were adopted

Which of these two illustrations shows an Anti-Corn Law League meeting, and which a Chartist meeting? What reasons do you have for making your choice?

which Cobden considered appropriate to "a middle-class set of agitators".

> *We have obtained the co-operation of the ladies,* he said; *we have resorted to tea parties.*[2b]

They also resorted to such events as Free Trade Fairs and the great bazaar held in Covent Garden Opera House in 1845 which might be called a forerunner of the Great Exhibition. In 1844 the League Council was in a position

> *to lend £20,000 to the Bolton Railway Company for twelve months at $3\frac{1}{2}\%$....*[1g]

With its efficient, business-like administration and ample funds, the League was, in the words of *The Times* of 18 November 1843,

> *a new power . . . arisen in the state.*[2a]

Nevertheless, it was realized that only through Parliament could the League's ends be achieved.

> *That House must be changed before we can get justice,*[1h]

said Cobden in a letter, and from 1843, the League set about trying to change it. They put constant pressure on M.P.s (something which was then considered unjustifiable interference with M.P.s' independence) and bombarded electors with publications. The country-wide organization already existing for the distribution of literature was able to provide up-to-date information on the electoral scene in each constituency. From 1843–45, the League exploited every loophole in the electoral law in order to object to the qualifications of protectionist voters and try to have their names struck off at the annual revision of registers. They met with some success and certainly caused their opponents much trouble. Some frivolous objections were made, as in the case of Peel whose vote at Tamworth was objected to, even though he was known to own almost the entire constituency! Leaguers also defended Free Trade votes and sought to create many more by urging Free Traders to purchase property carrying a vote. Here the 40s. freehold qualification was invaluable. The League organized the buying of property to be divided so as to produce a number of votes. It was estimated that £1¼ million was invested in such properties in three counties.

Such activities, while proving remarkably successful, involved immense expense in money and effort and achieved only limited results. The League also contested seats in by-elections—which did not endear them to the Whigs! There were difficulties, however, as Cobden pointed out:

> *We are in a most awkward predicament with the approaching vacancies—we can't find candidates—that's certain.*[1j]

The League, in fact, suffered some disastrous electoral defeats, largely because

> *... the returns are much more influenced by particular* local *circumstances than generally imagined ... the returns are greatly influenced by the* sufficiency *and* purse-weight *of* Candidates. . . .[1a]

But the presence of Cobden and Bright in the House of Commons was an invaluable asset, denied to the Chartists.

> *You speak with a loud voice when you are talking on the floor of the House; and if you have anything to say that hits hard, it is a very long whip and reaches all over the kingdom.[2b]*

One big difference usually noted between the Anti-Corn Law League and Chartism is that the League succeeded. But how much of the credit for repeal belongs to the League? Cobden conceded that

> *the League would not have carried the repeal of the Corn Laws when they did had it not been for the Irish famine and the circumstances that we had a Minister who thought more of the lives of the people than his own continuance in power.[2c]*

The League scarcely featured in the drama of the actual repeal. The votes Cobden controlled in the House in 1846 could never have brought it about and it is doubtful whether the League could ever have won enough support to carry repeal, but the legend of the League's victory has been perpetuated. In reality, Peel, though receptive to public opinion, pursued a policy which would eventually have led to repeal when he was convinced agriculture no longer needed the protection of the Corn Laws. Events in Ireland merely hastened the day.

In the long term, the League left its mark. Such was the power of its propaganda that the prosperity of the mid-century was attributed unhesitatingly to the effects of Free Trade. The belief in the benefits of Free Trade made protectionist measures unthinkable in the agricultural depression of the 1870s and lasted into the twentieth century.

The efforts of the League had also forced the ruling class to open its ranks, slowly and slightly, to the representatives of the rising commercial interests, thus carrying a step further the gains made in 1832.

[1a]from *Charter of the Nations* by Dunckley, quoted in *The Anti-Corn Law League* by Norman McCord (ALLEN & UNWIN, 1968); [1b]from *Manchester in 1844* by Leon Faucher, quoted in McCord, op. cit.; [1c]from Drake's *Road Book of the London and Birmingham and Grand Junction Railway of 1839*, quoted in McCord, op. cit.; [1d]P.R.O., H.O. 40/43, quoted in McCord, op.cit.; [1e]P.R.O., H.O. 40/54, quoted in McCord, op. cit.; [1f]from *Radical Leicester* by A. T. Patterson, quoted in McCord, op. cit.; [1g]letter

from Joseph Hickin to George Wilson in Wilson Papers, quoted in McCord, op. cit.; [1h]letter from Cobden in J. B. Smith's Corn Law Papers, quoted in McCord, op. cit.; [1j]letter from Cobden in Wilson Papers, quoted in McCord, op. cit.; [1k]letter from Joseph Parkes in Russell Papers, P.R.O. 30/22, Box 3, quoted in McCord, op. cit.; [2a]*The Age of Improvement* by Asa Briggs (LONGMAN); [2b]from *The Life of Richard Cobden*, Vol. I by Henry Morley, quoted in Briggs, op. cit.; [2c]from *Sixty Years of an Agitator's Life*, Vol. II by G. J. Holyoake, quoted in Briggs, op. cit.; [3]from the *Northern Star* 3 April 1841, quoted in *Free Trade and Protection* by Barry Turner (LONGMAN, 1971); [4]*A Social and Economic History of Britain* by Pauline Gregg (HARRAP, 1973).

Part Three
Continuity and Change

1. Upper and Middle Classes

In January 1868, Queen Victoria wrote to the Prince of Wales:

... there is one great danger, and one which it is the duty of all to try to avert, or the result may be very disastrous. This danger lies not in the power given to the Lower Orders, who are daily becoming more well-informed and more intelligent, and who will deservedly work themselves up to the top by their own merits, labour and good conduct, but in the conduct of the Higher Classes and of the Aristocracy.

Many, many with whom I have conversed, tell me that at no time for the last 60 or 70 years was frivolity, the love of pleasure, self-indulgence, luxury and idleness (producing ignorance) carried to such an excess as now in the Higher Classes, and that it resembles the time before the first French Revolution; and I must—alas!—admit that this is true. *Believe me! It is* most alarming, *although you do not observe it, nor will you hear it; but those who do not live in the gay court circle of fashion, and who view it calmly, are greatly, seriously alarmed. And in THIS lies the REAL* danger *of the* present time!

The Aristocracy and the Higher Classes must take great care, or their position may become very dangerous. I shall do what I can in this direction, but as you mix much with the gay and fashionable, you can do more, and so can dear Alix, to whom I wish you to show this letter, as I have often talked to her on these subjects.[1]

Nevertheless, by 1867, the power and influence of the upper class in Parliament and Government appeared virtually unchanged. The majority of seats in the House of Commons were still held by the landed class—a continuity which was now by courtesy of the middle classes and frequently as a result of concessions to their interests: for example, through the bringing of a railway or regulating of tolls on a canal, at local level, and attention to the needs of an industrial economy, at national level. Earl Grey's reference of 1831 to

> *the middle classes who form the real and efficient mass of public opinion,*
> *and without whom the power of the gentry is nothing*[2]

was equally true thirty years later.

Thus in 1867 the upper class retained the appearance of power and seemed unlikely to be ousted until redistribution of seats took place. But from 1868 onwards, increasing pressure from the middle classes brought the flood of legislation under Gladstone and Disraeli until by 1885

> *the number of commercial men and manufacturers in the House of Commons*
> *was greater than the number of landowners.*[3]

It did not come to a confrontation between landed and commercial interests because the change was gradual and landed interest possessed leaders skilled in compromise. Alexander Baring, Tory spokesman of 1831, had feared that

> *in a Reformed Parliament, when the day of battle came, the country*
> *Squires would not be able to stand against the active, pushing, intelligent*
> *people who could be sent from the manufacturing districts.*[2]

He was right, but the day of battle never came—the transference of power was effected without violence.

Fortunes fluctuated, as always, among the various families. Some continued to benefit from exploitation of industrial resources or the possession of city properties. Much of what they made was required to keep their estates going, for investment in land improvement often yielded no immediate return and eventually very little, seldom more than $2\frac{1}{2}\%$ when $3\frac{1}{2}\%-4\frac{1}{2}\%$ was

> *the interest a man can get for the mere use of his capital upon good*
> *securities, without adding a fraction of labour.*[4]

Many talked of giving up their estates and employing their capital more profitably:

> *What an infernal bore is landed property. No certain income can be*
> *reckoned upon.*[5a]
>
> *I do not think it worth while to keep a security paying 2%, when I can get*
> *an equally good one paying 5.*[5b]

On the other hand,

> *it would "pay" a millionaire in England to sink half his fortune in buying*
> *10,000 acres of land to return a shilling per cent, and live on the remainder,*
> *rather than to live upon the whole without land. He would be a greater*
> *person in the eyes of more people.*[5c]

The ownership of land conferred status.

Although many of the new rich came to be absorbed into the landed class, domestic and sporting habits continued in the traditional way. Patronage in the public service had ended by 1870—it was against the feeling of the time and the amateur had to make way for the professional—but in 1878 it was claimed that the professions, the Church, the Army and the Civil Service were still recruited largely from the landed interest who also preserved control in county government—even after 1888 many landowners were elected to the new county councils. The character of the Bench changed little, most magistrates being gentry or clergy. Similarly, the same men tended to be elected to serve on, for example, School Boards after 1870 but their powers in local affairs were largely curtailed by the increasing number of professional appointments—Police officers, Union (workhouse) officials, Inspectors of Schools. They still, however, held the prestige, if not the power.

There was much house-building by the well-to-do in the mid-century. The following table of prices appeared in a book by an eminent architect:

Proposed Outlay	Family Department			Servants' Department		
London (The Country)	Rooms	Average Height	Average Price	Rooms	Average Height	Average Price
£1,250 (£850 up)	13	12'	£68	13	11'3"	£28
£2,500 (£1,750 up)	20	12'9"	£90	19	11'7"	£37
£5,000 (£3,500 up)	30	13'9"	£121	29	12'	£47
£10,000 (£7,000 up)	45	15'	£163	43	12'6"	£62
£20,000 (£14,000 up)	67	16'6"	£220	65	13'	£80
£40,000 (£28,000 up)	100	18'	£298	97	13'6"	£105
£80,000	150	19'	£400	145	13'6"	£137

Stables and grounds cost extra!

Claremont Terrace, Glasgow, 1852

Primarily, the House of an English gentleman is divisible into two depart-
ments; namely, that of the Family and that of the Servants . . . as the im-
portance of the family increases, the distinction is widened—each depart-
ment becoming more and more amplified and elaborated in a direction con-
trary to that of the other . . . whether in a small house or a large one, let the
family have free passageway without encountering the servants unexpectedly
and let the servants have access to all their duties without coming unexpec-
tedly upon the family or visitors. On both sides this privacy is highly valued.[6]

Many modern facilities were, of course, still lacking, for gas
lighting was not in general use till the incandescent mantle came in in
the 1880s, nor was there electricity yet. Bathrooms were limited in
number, and hot water had usually to be carried upstairs by toiling
maids. Coal fires provided heat for some and work for others. A multi-
tude of petticoats served to protect legs from swirling draughts. The
Victorian family circle may have grouped closely round the fire more
from the need to keep warm than from delight in each other's company!

A continuing ample supply of servants, however, waited upon
the leisured classes. Ladies' maids dressed their mistresses in the elabor-
ate styles created, at the expense of health and eyesight, by ill-paid
seamstresses, often working in overcrowded, poorly-ventilated conditions. Dresses had to be hand-sewn till the advent of the sewing
machine, invented about 1851 but only adopted slowly because of the
availability of cheap labour.

The *Report on The Sanitary Circumstances of Dressmakers and other*
Needlewomen in London found in 1863 that

the ordinary hours of work are from ten to twelve hours, exclusive of meal
times. But . . . the hours of work are much lengthened during the Season
when *the earliest time of quitting work is 10 or 11 o'clock and under the*
pressure of court ceremonials, the work is often carried on far into the night.
Salaries for those who had served an unpaid apprenticeship of two
years might be £6, £8 or £10 per annum. If promoted after several
years' experience, a girl might earn £20–£25. Conditions, of course,
varied greatly.

Dressmakers, giving evidence to the Children's Employment
Commission in 1864, alleged that

the great cause of these long hours is that no one will refuse an order; they
make a promise for any time a lady wishes. I remember a dress ordered at
12, fitted on at 6 p.m., finished the same night, and sent home the first thing
next day. The lady who ordered it said "I suppose you work till 11, and
begin at 6 in the morning." She did not care how long we worked. We were
very much hurt at the way in which it was said.[7]

THE HAUNTED LADY, OR "THE GHOST" IN THE LOOKING-GLASS.
Madame La Modiste. "WE WOULD NOT HAVE DISAPPOINTED YOUR LADYSHIP, AT ANY SACRIFICE, AND THE ROBE IS FINISHED À MERVEILLE."

Upper-class women had adopted extravagant styles to distinguish themselves from those of lesser rank. Ironically, however, various factors contributed to enable the lower orders to imitate their betters. Plentiful materials, the sewing machine, the appearance of paper patterns and the beginnings of department stores and "ready-made" clothing all favoured the fashion-conscious working girl.

CRINOLINE FOR DOMESTIC USE.
Missus. "MARY! GO AND TAKE OFF THAT THING, DIRECTLY! PRAY, ARE YOU AWARE WHAT A RIDICULOUS OBJECT YOU ARE?"

The increase in the number of servants employed between 1851 and 1871 is an indication of the increasing prosperity of the middle classes in this period. The census figures for England and Wales show the following:

	1851	1861	1871	'51–'61	'61–'71	'51–'71
					% increase	
General Servants	575,162	644,271	780,040	12·0	21·0	35·6
Housekeepers	46,648	66,406	140,836	42·4	112·1	201·9
Cooks	44,009	77,822	93,067	76·8	19·6	111·5
Housemaids	49,885	102,462	101,505	105·9	7·8	121·5
Nursemaids	35,937	67,785	75,491	88·6	11·4	110·1
Laundrymaids	—	4,040	4,538	—	12·3	—
Totals	751,641	962,786	1,204,477	28·1	29·3	56·6
Population percentage increase				11·9	13·2	26·7
Population increase by separate families[8a]				21·0	12·4	36·0

Not only are the total increases interesting but it is significant that a big expansion has come in the employment of higher servants, like housekeepers and cooks, while the rise in the numbers of housemaids may indicate the addition of extra maids beyond the minimum desirable complement of three female servants.

It would also seem that more families were able to keep their own carriage, thus entering the upper-middle-class income bracket.

	1851	1861	1871	'51–'61	'61–'71	'51–'71
Indoor general servants (male)	74,323	62,076	68,369	− 16·5	− 10·1	− 8·0
Grooms	15,257	21,396	21,202	+ 40·2	− 0·9	+ 39·0
Coachmen	7,030	11,897	16,174	+ 69·2	+ 36·0	+ 130·1
Totals	96,610	95,369	105,745	− 1·3	+ 10·9	+ 9·5
Increase in number of households[8a]				21·0	12·4	36·0

These figures must be treated with caution, since grooms sometimes performed duties indoors and coachmen on occasion acted as grooms. The totals, therefore, are a more reliable guide. This increase in numbers also comes at a time of apparent increase in cost of purchase and keep of horses and in spite of the concurrent development of rail travel.

The number of passengers carried by the railways increased steadily throughout the nineteenth century.

Doll makers

Doll breakers

C.J. Staniyd.

1842	23 millions
1847	51 ,,
1851	79 ,,
1860	160 ,,
1880	604 ,,
1890	817 ,,
1913	1,455 ,,

Not only did the middle class use trains for travel to work but also for the annual holiday which was becoming recognized among the increasing number of salaried workers, many of whom had a paid vacation varying according to their length of service.

The 1851 census listed "watering-places" separately—they had a surprising annual growth rate. The sample fifteen included four spas and eleven resorts.

Annual growth rate—1851

Watering-places	2·561%
Manufacturing towns	2·380%
Mining and hardware towns	2·336%
Seaports	2·191%
London	1·820%
County towns	1·609%

Macauley described the watering-places as

the towns in which wealth, created and accumulated elsewhere, is expended for the purposes of health and recreation.[9]

Emphasis was placed on the value to health of "excursions" which were usually budgeted for along with items such as "doctors' fees", if indeed they were mentioned at all in the advice on expenditure in early works on domestic economy. However, an unknown sum obviously must have been set aside in this period for this purpose. The resorts grew in size and population, especially after rail links were established, and in provision of facilities for the visitors. Whereas the eighteenth-century visitors had been upper class, carrying on their usual life style while, in addition, drinking the waters and sea-bathing, the new nineteenth-century clientèle was mainly middle class, accompanied by their children. Some might still bring their servants to a hired house or lodgings but others patronized the large new hotels with their high standards of family comfort.

By 1875 it was true to say:

Complaints about the increase in the cost of living have of late been rife in every quarter.[8b]

Estimates varied up to 50%. In 1861 it was stated that

our parents, and certainly our grandparents, lived on half our means with nearly the same amount of comfort. And yet the positive price of the necessaries, certainly the luxuries of life, has not increased.[8c]

By painstaking research into the limited and very varied evidence available, it has been concluded that, though retail prices had only risen by 5% between 1850 and 1870 and servants' wages by less than 30%, an increased outlay of 50% on housekeeping generally was felt to be necessary in the 1870s to preserve the same standard of life.

A writer in 1875 put it this way:

It is a universal complaint . . . that life to a vast proportion of the middle classes is becoming more difficult and more costly. . . . Increased riches among high and low has brought increased demand for most articles, and in those articles consumption has overtaken production, and many of these are articles of prime necessity. Some of these can be brought from abroad, and the price of them has not, therefore, risen in proportion, if at all. But meat and all farm produce has risen so as to cause serious inconvenience in most families, and actual privation in many. House-rent and servants' wages, and servants' maintenance, have also risen most materially. With the general advance on the wages of labour in all trades, on which we have been congratulating the country, the cost of most articles into which labour enters largely as an element has been materially enhanced; and we have to pay more than we used to do for every job we want done. Probably, on the whole, we are within the mark if we say that, among average middle-class families, the actual cost of living is 25% higher than it was twenty-five years ago.

But this is only half the story. Owing to the increasing wealth of the wealthy, and the increasing numbers who every year step into the wealthier class, the style of living as well as the cost of necessaries and comforts of which "living" consists, has advanced in an extraordinary ratio; and however frugal, however unostentatious, however rational we may be, however resolute to live as we think we ought, and not as others do around us, it is, as we shall find, simply impossible not to be influenced by their example and to fall into their ways, unless we are content either to live in remote districts or in isolated fashion. The result is that we need many things that our fathers did not, and that for each of these many things we must pay more. Even where prices are lower, quantities are increasing. Locomotion is cheaper; but the middle-class family travels far more than formerly. Wine and tea cost less, but we habitually consume more of each.[8d]

Education was another item on which middle-class families were spending more. The lower middle class wanted sufficient education to allow their sons to enter "respectable" occupations, principally as clerks in City offices:

> *Parents are eager to get their sons into houses of business where they may maintain the appearance, if not the standing, of gentlemen.*[8e]

The attitude of farmers tended to be rather more indifferent:

> *The only spur which goaded them into a languid activity was the growing consciousness that their labourers were being better educated than their own sons.*[8f]

The upper middle class, however, had a positive interest in secondary education:

> *Relieved from the enervating influences of luxury, on the one hand, and the depressing influence of poverty, on the other; conscious that its retention of the advantages which it enjoys is still dependent on the mental activity by which they were gained; and keenly alive to aesthetic and intellectual pleasures, the upper middle class seems the least likely of all to neglect its own educational concerns.*[8g]

It became the educational concern of professional men and the wealthier industrialists to see their sons share the education of a gentleman which upper-class boys obtained at the public schools.

> *Gentleman,* Hippolyte Taine commented,—*these three syllables . . . summarize the history of English society.*[10]

Anthony Trollope could give no definition, but thought

> *any one would know what it meant,*[11]

while Samuel Smiles wrote that

> *they know each other instinctively.*[12]

Thomas Arnold told the scholars at Rugby School:

> *What we must look for here is, first, religious and moral principles; secondly, gentlemanly conduct; thirdly, intellectual ability.*

He wrote:

> *It is not necessary that this should be a school for three hundred, or even one hundred, boys, but it IS necessary that it should be a school of Christian gentlemen.*[13]

Commenting on the mixing of the classes, the old and new ruling groups, Matthew Arnold could say:

> *. . . it is only in England that this beneficial, inter-mixture of classes takes place. Look at the bottle-merchant's son and the Plantagenet being brought up side by side. None of your absurd separations and seventy-two quarterings here. Very likely young Bottles will end up by being a lord himself.*[14]

Later in the nineteenth century, A. C. Benson maintained that the public schools turned out

> *well-groomed, well-mannered, rational, manly boys, all taking the same view of things, all doing the same things.*[14]

Between 1840 and 1870, thirty-five new public schools were founded, in answer to increasing demand. The extension of the railway made it easier to send boys away to school and the old public schools had been reformed by eminent headmasters. In addition, the recognized method of entry to most branches of the Civil Service and to the Army, by 1870, was by competitive examination.

> . . . *human beings are no longer born to their place in life . . . but are free to employ their faculties, and such favourable chances as offer, to achieve the lot which may appear to them most desirable.*[15]

The public schools' emphasis on the Classics meant that they occupied 75% or more of the timetable. Maths was virtually ignored, French was usually an option and English had no real place. The new exams, however, were to test general education, giving a choice from a list of subjects. The Indian Civil Service offered: English and English History, 1500 marks; Classics (or Indian Classical language), 1500 marks; French, German, Italian, (each) 375 marks; Mathematics, 1250 marks; Natural Sciences, 500 marks; Logic, Mental and Moral Philosophy, 500 marks; Sanskrit, Arabic, (each) 375 marks. To discourage "cramming" and "smatterers", 125 marks were deducted from the total in each paper.

In response to the demands of the new exams—and of parents —some of the schools reluctantly introduced a "modern side". Thring, Head Master of Uppingham, stated the case:

> *The question of professional training remains. It has been shown . . . to be absolutely impossible to direct the studies of a great school to this end beyond a certain degree, without destroying the object of a great school which is, mental and bodily training in the best way, apart from immediate gain.*[16]

He showed his opinion of the "extra subjects" now being demanded— in them

> *the most backward in Classical knowledge can take refuge.*[16]

In the public schools, too, the popularity of "character-building" was established by the 1850s. Character, said Lord John Russell, was

> *much more important than the acquisition of mere knowledge.*[16]

Thus, in 1857, the *Saturday Review* observed:

> *We do not suppose that anyone hesitates to admit the great importance of keeping the proficiency of schoolboys in manly exercises up to the highest possible pitch. It is in these sports that the character of the boy is formed. It is from them that the readiness, pluck and self-dependence of the English gentleman are principally caught.*

By 1864, an average of fifteen hours a week was spent on cricket at Harrow. A master at Rugby could say of cricket:

> The discipline and reliance on one another, which it teaches, are so valuable. . . . It merges the individual in the eleven; he doesn't play that he may win but that his side may.[17]

Surveying the whole scene after a visit abroad in 1866, on behalf of the Schools Enquiry Commission, Matthew Arnold reported:

> So we have amongst us the spectacle of a middle class cut in two in a way unexampled anywhere else; of a professional class brought up on the first plane with fine and governing qualities but without the idea of science; while that immense business class, which is becoming so important a power in all countries, on which the future so much depends, and which in the leading schools of other countries fills so large a place, is in England brought up on the second plane, cut off from the aristocracy and the professions, and without governing qualities.[16]

Scottish education does not, of course, fit into the above pattern. The provision of secondary education was very much better. The Argyll Commission reported in 1868 1 in 140 receiving secondary education if private schools were included, otherwise 1 in 205. The figures for Prussia were 1 in 249, for France 1 in 570 and for England 1 in 1300. Scotland, with its population about one-sixth of the size of England's, had had four universities since the Middle Ages. By 1862, 1 in 869 attended a university, compared with around 1 in 2600 in Germany and 1 in 5800 in England. In addition, about 20% of students appeared to come from working-class backgrounds according to spot checks made in 1866 by the Commission who remarked that Scottish university education was "*not confined to a class, as in England*. . . ." The traditional Scottish Arts degree was based on a broad curriculum of the "modern" kind and the universities also provided highly successful professional training in medicine, law, engineering and science.

There was hardly any advance as yet in education for women. Pioneers like Elizabeth Blackwell and Elizabeth Garrett met with indignant opposition when they tried to enter the world of medicine. Many men and women echoed the Queen's words:

> What an awful idea this is—of allowing young girls and young men to enter the dissecting room together . . . to study things which could not be named before them.[18]

The breakthrough, however, was not far off.

Indeed, a blow had been struck for emancipation of women by Queen Victoria herself. She apparently did not accept the teaching in the Book of Genesis that "*in sorrow thou shalt bring forth children*" for she agreed to have, during the births of her last two babies,

that blessed Chloroform, and the effect was soothing, quieting and delightful beyond words.[18]

The Lancet of 14 May 1853 commented:

In no case could it be justifiable to administer Chloroform in perfectly natural labour,

but the Queen's anaesthetist, Dr John Snow, had written in 1847:

. . . where the pain is not greater than the patient is anxious to bear cheerfully, there is no occasion to use Chloroform; but when the patient is anxious to be spared the pain, I can see no valid objection to the use of this agent even in the most favourable cases.[18]

Since *"Royal examples are followed with extraordinary readiness"*, many women had cause to be grateful to their Queen.

[1]*King Edward VII* by Philip Magnus (PENGUIN, 1975); [2]*Politics in the Age of Peel* by N. Gash (LONGMAN); [3]*Elections and Party Management* by H. J. Hanham (LONGMAN); [4]from *Bankers Magazine*, XX, 1860, quoted in *Bankers and Pashas* by D. Landes (HEINEMANN, 1958); [5a]Lord Monson, quoted in *English Landed Society in the Nineteenth Century* by F.M.L. Thompson (ROUTLEDGE & KEGAN PAUL, 1971); [5b]Evelyn Denison, quoted in Thompson, op. cit.; [5c]from *The Economist*, 16 July 1870, quoted in Thompson, op. cit.; [6]*The Gentleman's House* by Robert Kerr (JOHNSON REPRINT CORPORATION, N.Y., 1972); [7]from Children's Employment Commission 2nd report, Vol. XXII, 1864, quoted in *Human Documents of the Victorian Golden Age* by E. Royston Pike (ALLEN & UNWIN, 1974); [8a]*Prosperity and Parenthood* by J. A. Banks (ROUTLEDGE & KEGAN PAUL 1954); [8b]from *The Cornhill Magazine*, April 1875, quoted in Banks, op. cit.; [8c]from *The Family Friend*, May 1861: "High Living with Low Means", quoted in Banks, op. cit.; [8d]from *Contemporary Review*, March 1876: "Life at High Pressure" by W. R. Grey, quoted in Banks, op. cit.; [8e]from *What Shall My Son Be? Hints to Parents on the Choice of a Profession or Trade* by F. Davenant, 1870, quoted in Banks, op. cit.; [8f]from *Royal Commission on Secondary Education: Report on Devon* by H. T. Geirans, 1895, quoted in Banks, op. cit.; [8g]from the *Edinburgh Review*, April 1876: "Secondary Education in Scotland", quoted in Banks, op. cit.; [9]*Englishman's Holiday* by J. A. R. Pimlott (HARVESTER PRESS, 1976); [10]*Notes on England* by Hippolyte Taine (BOOKS FOR LIBRARIES, INC., N.Y., 1957); [11]*Autobiography* by Anthony Trollope (OXFORD UNIV. PRESS, 1950); [12]*Self-Help* by Samuel Smiles (SPHERE, 1970); [13]Address to the Scholars at Rugby School by Thomas Arnold; [14]*Victorian People* by Asa Briggs (UNIV. OF CHICAGO PRESS, 1975); [15]J. S. Mill, quoted in *The Victorian Frame of Mind, 1830–1870* by W. E. Houghton (YALE UNIV. PRESS, 1957); [16]*Professional Men* by W. J. Reader (WEIDENFELD & NICOLSON, 1966); [17]*Tom Brown's Schooldays* by Thomas Hughes (PENGUIN, 1971); [18]*Victoria R. I.* by Elizabeth Longford (WEIDENFELD & NICOLSON, 1973).

2. Working Classes

In many ways the rural scene had changed little since 1837. Wages were still very low and in some senses were dropping since men often found that they were expected to do more work for the same money. Technology was beginning to make more impact on agriculture. Fertilisers were used extensively and greater use was made of machinery, but most work was done with traditional hand tools. In harvesting, for example, the sickle was still used, and young children plaited straw for binding sheaves. Although the labourer's position was unimproved, agriculture was expanding and 1869 was the year when the greatest acreage was under cultivation.

The working day lasted from dawn till sunset and at times beyond that. One woman later recalled how in harvest time

we worked together setting up the shocks by moonlight.[1]

The ploughboy usually started work fully an hour before dawn, feeding and preparing the horses for the day's work. He was often about ten years old and would spend the day tramping the fields with

two or three pounds of dirt to his boots, all thrown in for sixpence a day.[2a]

Child labour was used extensively on farms and often involved long hours, especially in the "gangs" which were hired to do specific tasks for farmers. Other children might be employed to scare birds, and one mother told a commission that her nine year old son had worked from 4 a.m. till 7 p.m. seven days a week, alone in a field. For this he received 4d. a day. It was 1867 before any investigation was made into the employment of young children in the country, and although legislation controlling the "gang" system was then passed, it had little effect, partly because the magistrates, as employers, wanted the children's labour, and partly because the families were so poor that they needed the wages which the children brought in.

Despite these poor conditions, agricultural labourers made no real effort to organize a union at this time. A *Morning Chronicle* reporter broached this subject with a farm labourer in 1850 and was told:

We are too much in their [the employers'] power for that. If any man complains they call him sausy and discharge him at once.[3]

By the 1860s, Professor Beesly was taking a more optimistic view and foretold:

Agricultural labourers have as strong a motive as others [for forming trade unions], but they have not the opportunity. Nevertheless, even they will some day benefit by the experience, and, it may be, the direct aid of the skilled labourers, and it will be amusing then to watch the consternation of certain philanthropic noblemen and gentlemen who now look so sharp after the manufacturers with Ten Hours' Bills, Bills for fencing machinery, whitewashing factories, fixing dinner hours, etc., while the cottages on their own estates are nests of consumption, typhus and incest.[4]

Like the hours and conditions of work, housing in the rural areas was in much the same state in 1867 as it had been thirty years earlier. The Duke of Bedford had said in 1851:

To improve the dwellings of the labouring class, and afford them the means of greater cleanliness, health and comfort in their own homes, to extend education and thus raise the social and moral habits of those most valuable members of the community, are among the first duties, and ought to be among the truest pleasures, of every landlord.[5a]

Certainly the Duke did provide good housing at a low rent for his permanent workers; but temporary labourers still lived either in the slums of "open" villages or in their own ramshackle houses. If it was uneconomic to build workers' houses in towns, then it was even less economic to do so in the country where the wages were lower and the work less certain. The result was the kind of slum described by a clergyman in 1867:

They are deficient in bedroom accommodation, . . . in drainage and sanitary arrangements; they are imperfectly supplied with water; such conveniences as they have are often so situated as to become nuisances; they are full enough of draughts to generate any amount of rheumatism; and in many instances they are lamentably dilapidated and out of repair.[6a]

No investigation into the conditions of housing in the country areas took place till 1885 and then one witness described a "good" house as one with sound floor, walls, roofs and windows which kept out the weather. He added that he knew of no part of rural Britain in which such houses were common.

Diet also contributed to the general misery. For most families it was simple and slight. One investigator reported:

For years past their daily diet is potatoes for breakfast, dinner and supper and potatoes only,[7a]

E

THE COTTAGE.

Mr. Punch (to Landlord). "YOUR STABLE ARRANGEMENTS ARE EXCELLENT! SUPPOSE YOU TRY SOMETHING OF THE SORT HERE! EH?"

Model farm buildings, Longleat

while Joseph Arch, who was later to found a union for farm labourers, remembered that in his childhood

> ... *even the barley loaves were all too scarce.* ... *The food we could get was of very poor quality, and there was far too little of it. Meat was rarely, if ever, to be seen on the labourer's table.* ... *In many a household even a morsel of bacon was considered a luxury.*[7a]

Illnesses such as rheumatism and bronchitis were common, both from working outdoors in wet weather, and from lack of a change of clothing, and drying facilities at home. Labourers often went to work in the morning with clothes still wet from the previous day's rain.

One reform which improved health in rural areas was the 1853 Act making smallpox vaccination compulsory. Even this had its discomforts however, since vaccinated infants were often taken round the district and their scabs broken so that other children could be vaccinated from their wounds.

In rural areas there was even less chance of leisure than there was in the towns. Most children in country areas attended school, but there were frequent and prolonged absences while they helped with agricultural work. Nor was school devoted only to the Three Rs. In most rural schools emphasis was placed on "knowing his place in society", and children were sometimes punished in school for not curtseying or saluting a local landowner. Even so, some of the upper classes were not convinced that education for the rural worker was a good idea. In 1857 Bishop Wilberforce stated that

> *they did not want everyone to be learned men or to make everyone unfit for the plough, or else the rest of us would have nothing to eat.*[2b]

Such conditions explain Canon Girdlestone's comment that labourers *did not live in the proper sense of the word, they merely didn't die.*[7a]

Certainly the first half of Victoria's reign was one in which the upper urban working class had made some progress. Wages were about 40% higher in 1866 than they had been in 1840. Clerical posts were increasing in industry and provided means of progress for those children whose parents had invested in their education. For the skilled and intelligent workmen too, managerial posts and supervisory positions were increasing as fewer of the second or third generation of factory owners either wished, or were able, to run the family business. A very few women were also beginning to find employment in offices and this may have encouraged some parents to educate daughters as well as sons. Hours of work were by then shorter. Many trades were by 1867 working a ten and a half hour day, and usually work ended at 2 o'clock on Saturday. This, and the cheap travel which had become available especially in towns, was leading to a growth of interest in sport, and football clubs were beginning to appear.

Child labour was still a problem. The existing legislative restrictions applied only to certain types of employment. In 1861, a Royal Commission was set up at Lord Shaftesbury's instigation to enquire into the places of work in which children were employed. The reports came out between 1863 and 1866 and showed that many children were still employed in dangerous and arduous work. In potteries, nine-year old boys, sometimes working in temperatures of over 140° F, earned about 3s. per week. Others worked at match-making and this often caused "Phossy jaw" and death as a result of the phosphorous fumes eating away the teeth and jaw-bone. Others worked in foundries and were often burned by molten metal. Some young girls of twelve were found working in brickworks where they individually handled 36 tons of bricks in a day. Most pathetic of all were the climbing boys, who, despite earlier legislation, were still to be found from the age of four climbing chimneys and "sleeping black". These too often died young either from suffocation or lung diseases resulting from inhaling soot.

Attempts had been made to improve the housing of the working classes in towns, but little had been achieved. The main problem throughout the century was that the urban population grew rapidly, mainly because of the steady flow of rural labourers attracted by the higher wages. There was also an influx of Irish and Highlanders resulting from the potato famine and Clearances respectively. All of this meant that although food and clothing prices dropped during this period, the rent of houses rose steadily, and by 1867 it was reckoned that about half the urban working class was paying between quarter and half of its income on rent. Local authorities could demolish slum property but few did. Most demolition resulted from road and railway construction, and even when there was rebuilding of houses, the rents were much higher, and outwith the reach of the evicted. One reason for this was that some regulations had been introduced to raise the standard of housing. A certain amount of space had to be provided around houses, cellars could not be used as dwellings, and all houses had to have lavatories and sinks. Many builders began to include kitchen ranges and ovens, but all of these improvements raised the cost of house building to such an extent that it was necessary to rent them at a price which no poor family could afford. The result was even greater overcrowding in the slum areas which remained. In Glasgow in the 1860s,

A Glasgow wynd, 1868

5% of the families lived in single rooms and also had a lodger.

There were many who did try to help. Octavia Hill began by acquiring nine houses in a slum area. All were overcrowded but to some extent this problem was solved since

those who would not pay, or who led clearly immoral lives were ejected.[6b]

Those who remained were encouraged to take more accommodation as it became available, and repairs and redecoration were undertaken. This venture was successful in that those who were housed became more satisfactory tenants although during rent collection there were

sometimes rebukes for untidiness to be administered.[6c]

A 5% profit was also gained which could be used for repairs and improvements. The various attempts at model housing during this period all tried to show a profit to encourage more investment, but greater and quicker profits were made by investment in business. The rules of behaviour were also very much a part of such schemes and these deterred many of the working class from entering these houses. They preferred the greater freedom of the slums rather than the better housing where they had to obey middle-class standards.

Many families were spending more on food by the 1860s, despite the fact that food prices had dropped 12% since 1845. The food bought, however, was usually of a low standard. Improvements in transportation did mean that milk and vegetables could be brought more quickly to the urban centres, and this brought greater variety to the working-class diet. Adulterated food was still common. Tea was one commodity which was investigated by scientists during this time. They found that

> the facing from the sample of black tea was perfectly black in colour, and on examination was found to consist of earthy graphite, or black lead.[7b]

Beer was just as unhealthy since after diluting it with water, publicans were in the habit of adding a little vitriol

> to bring up a head.[7c]

These additions were deliberate but there were others which resulted from lack of hygiene, especially in bakers' premises. One inspector reported:

> The principal fact, for which I was certainly not prepared was their extreme dirt, and in many places the almost total covering of the entire space between the rafters with masses of cobwebs, weighed down with flour dust that had accumulated upon them, and hanging in strips just above your head. A heavy tread or a blow upon the floor above, brought down large fragments . . . masses of these cobwebs must be frequently falling into the dough.[6d]

Despite articles in *The Lancet* it was not till 1875 that any action was taken to control adulteration.

One body which did much to raise the standard of working-class food was the Co-operative Movement, but this was an uphill task since many of their customers preferred the brighter colours of the adulterated foods. By the 1860s co-operatives were beginning to amalgamate to buy foods wholesale and this reduced their prices even more.

Public health was another area in which improvements had taken place. This was largely the result of Edwin Chadwick's efforts. One reason for this growth of interest was that diseases such as cholera could attack the wealthy as well as the poor. *The Times* summed up this attitude when it said in 1848:

The cholera is the best of all sanitary reformers.[8]

When the epidemics passed there was a sudden drop in interest since improvements cost money and local authorities were always unwilling to spend more than was necessary. This attitude led Hole to write:

As a means of improving the conditions of our towns, it would be very desirable to improve the character of the local bodies who conduct its (sic) affairs. . . . An improvement will be voted against, that the rival factions may show which has the greater zeal for "economy". If a nuisance or an abuse has to be defended, it will not want defenders.[5b]

It was such councillors who caused the commission into local government which started in 1868 and which eventually led to the Public Health Act of 1875.

Some authorities were more enthusiastic, or more frightened than others. Liverpool, Glasgow and the City of London were quick to appoint Medical Officers of Health, and in these cities there was a gradual reduction in the death rate from fevers, diarrhoea, cholera and smallpox. But such officers could do nothing to prevent overcrowding which was still a major factor in the spread of disease. Reports of up to 15 people living in one room came from Dr Russell of Glasgow and, as he pointed out:

Living in such a state of aggregation, it is not surprising to find the state of the person in general most disgusting. . . .[9a]

This was helped in some places by local authorities assuming responsibility for the water supply and although the initial outlay was considerable, the water supply was purer, cheaper and more regular thereafter.

One of the greatest problems faced by those who were attempting to improve the health of town dwellers was the lack of trained medical personnel. This was particularly true of nurses. Despite the work of Florence Nightingale, nursing in general was still an untrained job. The standard of recruit was low, so much so that Dr Russell complained in his 1866 report:

I often fancy people are amused while listening to my complaints, and surprised that I have not yet learned to believe that drink and dishonesty are essential properties of a nurse. I admit that at present nursing is the last resource of female adversity. . . . When on a rare occasion a respectable young woman takes to it from choice, her friends most likely repudiate her. . . . The Matron has met instances of this, of friends saying, "Surely your character is lost, or you would not be in a place like this".[9b]

The statistics of nurses employed in the fever hospital in Glasgow over a two year period prove that the public estimation of nurses was not far wrong. Out of thirty-five employed, seven were dismissed for drinking, five for inefficiency, four for dishonesty, one for ill-using patients, and six left of their own accord, of whom Dr Russell said:

> *Glad to be rid of some of them.*[9b]

Until this situation was changed there was little benefit to be gained from the many medical advances being made by Lister, Simpson and others.

In other ways too, towns had changed by 1867. From almost the beginning of Victoria's reign, police forces had reduced crime considerably. Reformatory schools replaced prisons for boys convicted for the third time. There they were detained for about two years and taught a craft, in addition to being given a basic education. This certainly reduced the number of juvenile pick-pockets, whose previous wealth had acted as an attraction into crime for many urban youngsters. But as late as 1876, Dr Barnardo estimated that there were, in London alone, about 30,000 children under sixteen sleeping rough, and it was from these that the supply of young criminals usually came.

Many saw education as a means of reducing the crime which was so prevalent in Victorian towns, and increasingly efforts were made to provide some schooling for children. In 1862 the system of payment by results was instituted by the Government to raise the standard in those schools which received a Government grant. The most noticeable result of this was that the sum paid dropped from £813,000 in 1861 to £637,000 in 1865. A side-effect was the increased tension in schools at the time of the annual inspection, which determined the amount granted for the next year. One man later recalled that during the inspection of his school,

> *the boys howled and the girls whimpered. It took hours to get through them.*[2c]

J. S. Mill's assessment that the education provided by the National and British and Foreign Schools was

> *never good except by some rare accident and generally so bad as to be little more than nominal.*[10]

is supported by the evidence available. But literacy was increasing, perhaps stimulated by the flood of cheap reading materials which resulted from the abolition of the paper tax in 1861. To the disgust of reformers most of those who became literate showed a preference for the "penny dreadfuls" which immortalized Sweeney Todd and Dick Turpin, rather than improving themselves by serious study. The *Boys'*

Own Paper was started in competition to these sensational magazines.

More serious than this was the fact that thousands were still completely illiterate. In 1864, a Commission into the Employment of Children could find a witness who could say that he was

> ... *going on for 13. Have never been to day school; go to Sunday School sometimes. Never learned anything; can't read or write or do sums. Never heard of Edinburgh. Don't know where London is. ... I know about my own work and that is about all I know.*[11]

Even those who did attend schools learned nothing about technology or science, and with the growth of this kind of education on the Continent, Britain was in danger by 1867 of being left behind in the next stage of industrialization.

In conclusion, it was still possible to find in Britain in 1867 those who believed that

> *a numerous population ... is absolutely indispensable to the rich, if they would enjoy their riches, or increase them by honest means.*[4]

It was as a result of this attitude that, although Acts of Parliament were passed in 1788, 1834, 1840 and 1864 banning the use of boys as chimney sweeps, boys continued to be so employed and to die in this employment until 1875, mainly because the magistrates chose to ignore laws which did not suit them. It could still be asked in 1868:

> *What sort of progress is this, in which the larger part of the community remains as miserable, if not more miserable, than in a state of barbarism?*[12]

It was a society in which the top 0.07% of the population owned 16·2% of the income, and in which the bottom 9·9% received 2%.

But changes had taken place and the attitudes had developed which would lead to further changes within the next ten years. The bitterness of the earlier class struggle had largely disappeared. The upper working class, especially, was no longer fighting the employers but rather co-operating with them to improve its own position. One reason for the 1867 Reform Act was the Government's belief that the working class, in towns at least, had absorbed enough of middle-class attitudes to make it safe to give them the vote. The trade unions were regarded as sufficiently respectable to be given legal coverage of their funds in 1869 and the first official T.U.C. met in 1868 without revolution being preached. The Government was also starting to take the side of the working class on some issues. It could be said that

> *in little more than a decade [1868–78] the presumption of the law had shifted from trusting the industrialist to protect his workers unless he*

> *proved unworthy of the trust, to suspecting him of exploitation unless he was inspected by the state.*[13]

It was a sign of these changing attitudes that, when the trade unions obtained the amending of the Master and Servant Laws which had oppressed workers for so long, the revised version appeared as the Employer and Workman Act!

---

[1]*Village Life and Labour* ed. by R. Samuel (ROUTLEDGE & KEGAN PAUL, 1975); [2a]*The Victorian Country Child* by P. Horn (ROUNDWOOD PRESS, 1974); [2b]from *Oxfordshire Clergy 1777–1869* by D. McClatchy, quoted in Horn, op. cit.; [2c]from *Joseph Ashby of Tysoe* by M. K. Ashby, quoted in Horn, op. cit.; [3]*The Victorian Working Class* ed. by P. E. Razzell and R. W. Wainwright (FRANK CASS, 1973); [4]from the *Westminster Review*, Vol. XX, 1861, quoted in *Trade Unions in the Victorian Age*, Vol. III (GREGG INTERNATIONAL, 1974); [5a]from *English Architecture in 1850–51* by J. Caird, quoted in *Cruel Habitations* by Enid Gauldie (ALLEN & UNWIN, 1974); [5b]from *Homes of the Working Class* by J. Hole, 1866, quoted in Gauldie, op. cit.; [6a]from *Employment of Children, Young Persons and Women in Agriculture, 1867*, quoted in *Human Documents of the Victorian Golden Age* by E. Royston Pike (ALLEN & UNWIN, 1974); [6b]Royston Pike, op. cit.; [6c]from *Homes of the London Poor* by Octavia Hill, quoted in Royston Pike, op. cit.; [6d]from *Report on Grievances of Journeymen Bakers* by Tremenheere, 1862, quoted in Royston Pike, op. cit.; [7a]*Plenty and Want* by J. Burnett (PENGUIN, 1968); [7b]from *Memoirs of the Chemical Society*, 1851, quoted in Burnett, op. cit.; [7c]from *Report on the Select Committee on Public Houses*, quoted in Burnett, op. cit.; [8]*History of Public Health* by A. Swinson (WHEATON, 1965); [9a]*Analyses of 300 Cases of Typhus* by Dr James Russell, 1864, from Clean Bill of Health teaching kit; [9b]*Report of the City of Glasgow Fever Hospital* by Dr James Russell, 1866, as above; [10]*Laissez-Faire and State Intervention in Nineteenth-Century Britain* by Arthur J. Taylor (MACMILLAN, 1972); [11]*Labour's Formative Years* by J. B. Jefferys (LAWRENCE & WISHART, 1948); [12]*1868—The Year of the Unions* by E. Frow and M. Katanka (KATANKA, 1968); [13]*The Origins of Modern English Society 1780–1880* by H. Perkin (ROUTLEDGE & KEGAN PAUL, 1972).

Assignments

A. The tables on the following page are taken from *A Manual of Domestic Economy* by J. H. Walsh (1857, 1873). Study them carefully, then answer the following questions.

1. Find out what is meant by "Italian goods", greengrocery, chandlery.

2. Look at the individual items of the housekeeping budgets.

a. On which items do all income groups spend most?

b. Which items would you expect the lower income groups to cut out or cut down on?

c. Do they in fact do so?

3. Walsh gives the household sizes as follows:—

£100/£150—6 persons £250/£350 — 7 persons
£500/£750—9 persons £1,000/£1,500—11 persons

He takes the average family size to include 4 children.

a. Find out from the information in Chapter 1 who the other members of the households are likely to be.
Be as specific as you can.

b. You might think that expenditure on food for a household of 9 should be roughly $1\frac{1}{2}$ times that for a household of 6: feeding 11 people might cost about twice as much as feeding 6.
Look at *amounts* spent on items of food. These calculations only hold good for one item—which is it? What does this tell us about the diet of the lowest income group?

4. Copy out the following plan. Make the calculations and fill in the answers.

Table 1—1857

Income	£1,000	£500	£250	£100
Total spent on housekeeping				
Percentage of total income spent on housekeeping				
Total spent on food alone				

a. What are the implications for the lower income group of the fact that they have to spend such a large proportion of their income on food?

b. Work out the same details for the 1873 Table.

c. Walsh seems to imply that an income of 50% more is needed by 1873 to keep up the 1857 standard of living yet the estimated increase in food prices over the period is only 5%. Look at the *totals* spent on food in the two tables. What conclusion do you come to about the middle-class's consumption of food?

Table 1—1857

Income	£1,000		£500		£250		£100	
Housekeeping items	Amount £s	%*	Amount £s	%	Amount £s	%	Amount £s	%
Meat, bacon	75	21·4	40	20·0	30	20·0	18	27·7
Fish, poultry	30	8·6	10	5·0	7	4·7	—	—
Bread	20	5·7	16	8·0	14	9·3	10	15·4
Milk, butter, cheese	20	5·7	18	9·0	16	10·7	8	12·3
Grocery	30	8·6	20	10·0	18	12·0	8	12·3
Italian goods	8	2·3	5	2·5	3	2·0	—	—
Greengrocery	20	5·7	12	6·0	10	6·7	6	9·2
Beer	20	5·7	12	6·0	10	6·7	5	7·7
Wine, spirits	50	14·3	15	7·5	8	5·3	1	1·5
Coals	25	7·1	15	7·5	12	8·0	5	7·7
Chandlery	12	3·4	7	3·5	7	4·7	2	3·1
Washing	40	11·4	30	15·0	15	10·0	2	3·1

Table 2—1873

Income	£1,500		£750		£350		£150	
Housekeeping items	Amount £s	%	Amount £s	%	Amount £s	%	Amount £s	%
Meat, bacon	110	19·8	60	20·3	50	22·7	30	31·6
Fish, poultry	45	8·1	15	5·1	12	5·5	—	—
Bread	25	4·5	20	6·8	18	8·2	12	12·6
Milk, butter, cheese	25	4·5	22	7·5	20	9·1	10	10·5
Grocery	35	6·4	28	9·5	22	10·0	10	10·5
Italian goods	10	1·8	7	2·3	5	2·3	—	—
Greengrocery	25	4·5	15	5·1	12	5·5	8	8·4
Beer	25	4·5	15	5·1	12	5·5	8	8·4
Wine, spirits	80	14·4	20	6·8	10	4·5	1	1·1
Coals	40	7·2	25	8·5	20	9·1	10	10·5
Chandlery	20	3·6	10	3·4	9	4·1	3	3·2
Washing	50	9·0	40	13·6	30	13·6	3	3·2
Repairs and extras	65	11·7	18	6·1	—	—	—	—

*% = percentage of total housekeeping bill spent on each item

B.

In those spacious halls the benignant power of steam summons around him his myriads of willing menials, and assigns to each the related task, substituting for painful muscular effort on their part, the energies of his own gigantic arm, and demanding in return only attention and dexterity. (Philosophy of Manufactures: Ure.)

Perhaps it is not good when a factory girl, who has not the whole spirit of play spun out of her for want of meadows, gambols upon bags of wool, a little too near the exposed machinery that is to work it up, and is immediately seized and punished by the merciless machine that digs its shaft into her pinafore and hoists her up, tears out her left arm at the shoulder joint, breaks her right arm and beats her on the head. . . . Why do we talk about such horrible things? Because they exist, and their existence should be clearly known. Because there have occurred during the last three years, more than a hundred such deaths and more than ten thousand such accidents in our factories. . . . (Ground in the Mill: Henry Morley.)

    a. What different roles do the two authors assign to machines and workers?

    b. Which aspects of factory life does each stress?

    c. To what extent do either or both give a distorted picture of factory life?

C.

The preachers of the Manchester school, the apostles of self-help, . . . are not ashamed to talk of making money and getting on in the world, as if it were the whole duty of the working man. . . . But you who are working men, and have a little practical experience of the thing, you do not want me or anyone else to tell you that the men who raise themselves from the ranks are very often not distinguished by fine dispositions or even by great abilities. What is wanted for success of that sort is industry, perseverance, and a certain sharpness, often of a low sort. I am far from saying that those who raise themselves are not often admirable men; but you know very well that they are sometimes very much the reverse—and that they are morally inferior to the average workman who is content with his position and only desires that his work may be regular and his wages fair. (The Social Future of the Working Class: E. S. Beesly.)

The greatest results in life are usually obtained by simple means, and the exercise of ordinary qualities. The common life of every day, with its cares, necessities, and duties affords ample opportunity for acquiring experience of the best kind; and its most beaten paths provide the true worker with abundant scope for effort and room for self-improvement. The great high-road of human welfare lies along the old highway of steadfast well-doing; and they who are the most persistent, and work in the truest spirit, will invariably be the most successful. (Self-Help: Samuel Smiles.)

    a. On what points do Beesly and Smiles agree?
    b. On what points do they differ?
    c. Read both extracts again carefully. Write two short letters to the press in reply to these authors, either supporting or opposing their views, using your knowledge of this period to do so.

Putting Children First
A Volume in Honour of Mia Kellmer Pringle

Reproduced by kind permission of Times Newspapers Limited